YOUR PURPOSE WILL COST YOU EVERYTHING!

Purpose Letters - Volume 1
A 30-day devotional

Dr Samuel Ekundayo

YOUR PURPOSE WILL COST YOU EVERYTHING!

Copyright© 2025 | Dr Samuel Ekundayo

All rights reserved; no part of this publication may be reproduced, stored in a retrieval system or transmitted in any form or by any means electrical, mechanical, photocopying, recording or otherwise – without the prior written permission of the author or publisher.

The right of Dr Samuel Ekundayo to be identified as the author of this book has been asserted by him in
accordance with copyright laws.

ISBN: 981-1-7385992-7-1

For all information, address all correspondence to the author's webssite: www.samuelekundayo.com

DEDICATION

This book is dedicated to you dear reader. I pray that you will discover and fulfil the purpose of God for your life and be all He has created you to be in Jesus' name.

Amen!

I believe in you.

ACKNOWLEDGEMENTS

Firstly, I thank God for giving me the ability to write this book. Every opportunity to bless my generation through my writing give me so much fulfilment and I attribute that to the grace and gift of God.

To my Dudushewa and Treasure, I thank you for your consistent love, encouragement, and companionship. Thank you for believing in me and always rooting for me. I love you endlessly.

And to my parents (biological and spiritual), mentors and guides God has placed over me,

thank you for all you have done and still doing to stir me in the right direction. I will always be grateful.

Special thanks to my team of amazing and God-sent individuals God has used for me to write this book. Pastor Ayodele Mike for your help in rewriting the initial parts of the book; Pastor Sam Adetiran for helping me edit the book, and my beloved Opeoluwa Adebakin for the beautifully designed book cover.

Table of Contents

Day 1 : God Has Great Plans For You.................................8

Day 2 : It's Time To Awaken From Your Slumber...............15

Day 3 : How To Take Action From What You Have Learnt...... 21

Day 4: Is Your Fuse Blown?.. 28

Day 5: Sometimes You Win, Sometimes You Learn................. 33

Day 6: Lessons About Growth 38

Day 7: Be A Person Of Value 43

Day 8: Time Was Given For Purpose.............................. 48

Day 9: Knowledge Audit... 52

Day 10: Your Purpose Is Valid 55

Day 11: Begin Today! Start Now! 60

Day 12: Your Purpose Will Cost You Everything................. 64

Day 13: Success Leaves Clues... 68

Day 14: What Is Your One Thing? 73

Day 15: You Can Not Fulfill Purpose Alone.................... 75

Day 16: The Power Of Commitment............................... 81

Day 17: You May Not Feel Qualified 86

Day 18: Big Dreams Equal Big Price................................ 91

Day 19: No One Is Better Than You 94

Day 20: Availability 97

Day 21: The Power Of Words 100

Day 22: Be Mindful 106

Day 23: Stop Dabbling Into Things 109

Day 24: Envision Your Life As A Sport 114

Day 25: Don't Reject Knowledge 118

Day 26: Your Purpose Is Not Far From You 123

Day 27: The Altitude Of Greatness 127

Day 28: Value 130

Day 29: Success Is A Lifestyle 135

Day 30: The Power Of Relationships 138

DAY 1

GOD HAS GREAT PLANS FOR YOU

I was recently in North America on a leadership tour with my bosom friend, Dr Niyi Borire. On one of the days, we were preparing for our event in Houston – getting the hall we would be using ready, setting up the banners and all – when a young family walked towards us.

I noticed they were looking at us rather intently but didn't say anything. They walked by and a few minutes later, they came back.

The woman approached me and said, '*Excuse me, sir, I know you. You are the Purpose Preacher, the father of the purposeful brothers; your wife is Dudushewa.*'

The husband chimed in, and said, 'She's been telling me about you and your family.'

I was blown away that someone would recognise me halfway across the world.

Whereas this happens to me once in a while now, I still can't get over the fact that God chose a village boy like me to take His Word and name to nations.

Like in the words of David, '*Who am I, Sovereign LORD, and what is my family, that you have brought me this far?*'

Why am I sharing this with you?

God wants to use you greatly.

You cannot even imagine what He has in mind for you. He wants your impact and reach to touch nations of the earth.

Your books will go to places you may never reach. Your videos may touch lives you may never meet. Your prayers have the potential to affect destinies who may never meet you to say, 'Thank you.' Your products could be saving people who are hanging on for their dear lives.

This is what I preach to people, 'Don't hold anything back!' God has been gracious to give you everything you would need to influence and affect your world positively and the best you can do is to unleash your best to the world. One of the issues I do have with most people is that they don't know that their little gift to the world can greatly impact the world.

You are made something special, and God has plans for you, His plans for you are beautiful and great, and you are to take the responsibility of uncovering those plans of God for your life because God won't come down to do for you what you can do for yourself. You will have to rise and begin to intentionally live a purposeful life. God wants to take you to places, He wants to connect you with great opportunities out there, He wants to open great doors for you, but you have to walk in the path of His plans for your life.

'For I know the thoughts that I think toward you, says the Lord, thoughts of peace and not of evil, to give you a future and a hope.'
Jeremiah 29:11 NKJV.

God's plans for your life are the best, nothing can beat it or make it inferior. His plans are great. I never imagined that I could travel around the world and someone from afar, or people I don't even know would recognise me. Well, it's part of God's great plan for me. God also has plans for you and He wants you to seriously walk in the path of that plan. God wants to do things in your life that will leave your mouth open in awe. God wants to bless you. God wants to prosper you. God wants you to be favoured. God doesn't just want to bless you, He also wants to do great things through you. Those are His plans for your life, great isn't it?

I love how the Apostle Paul said it,

'Eye has not seen, nor ear heard,
Nor have entered into the heart of man

YOUR PURPOSE WILL COST YOU EVERYTHING!

The things which God has prepared for those who love Him.' 1 Corinthians 2:9 NKJV.

God has great things in store for you and He wants to use you for His glory and purpose.

Almost everyone in the world wants to discover God's divine plan for themselves, but they forget that God's plan cannot be found in every place, it can only be found in His presence. God's plan can't be in the University, you may be at the University for seven years as a student of medicine without discovering God's ultimate plan for your life. You may be at the law school for several years without knowing what God's plan for you is, but when you come to His presence, He uncovers the hidden truth about His plans for you.

This is why you must genuinely be saved so you can be in His presence. There are lots of people presently at Oxford University, Harvard Business School, and some of those prestigious schools without knowing what God's plan is for them. This is just to let you understand that you may go to the South, or travel to the West, but if you have not come back to God, His plans for you will be hidden.

God's plan for everyone is great, God's plan for you is great. The reason you are reading this right now is because God's plan for you is great. Discovering that plan solely depends on you, this is why you must come back to His presence. It is in His presence that those plans will be revealed and uncovered for you. God's plans for you are great and excellent. You may be going through some difficulties at the moment, but those difficulties would not in any way change God's plan for you. You may fail, and fall, that would not change His beautiful plans for you.

When Paul was Saul, he was busy persecuting the church; he was going about from one place to the other destroying churches. He thought he would do that for a long period, but unknown to him, God had a different plan. Amazingly, God would always use some of the most foolish things to confuse the wise. Yes, because God is unpredictable. You may be at a point in your life right now where nothing is working for you again, but that doesn't mean things won't work for you tomorrow. You may have financial crises right now and be in serious debt, but God's plan for you may make you a kingdom financier. Everything happening around your life, family, marriage, finances and even your career is happening because God has greater plans for you.

God's plans for you are beautiful and unfathomable. The only reason you are in despair is simply because you don't know what those plans are. If you understand what God has in plan for you, then you will rest assured that the future will be smooth for you.

He says, *'Be still, and know that I am God...'* Psalms 46:10 NKJV.

God will make your journey smooth, just rest in Him. Don't be afraid of what the future holds because the future holds greatness for you, there are so many pleasant surprises that are yet to be uncovered for you. They won't be uncovered yet, but as you get along with God, He will uncover those plans for you.

One of the reasons God has great plans for you is simply because you are not an afterthought, He was deliberate about creating you and He has put inside of you everything you will need for maximum impact. I want you to see the reasons why God intentionally created you. Stop looking at those unpleasant situations around you, just focus on God's plans.

I want you to begin to see the bigger picture of God's plan for your life because if you can just see them, you will get them, but if you refuse to see, it will be impossible for you to get them because you will always get what you see with your eyes. See God's plan as big as any mountain you have ever seen and if you haven't seen any mountain, see God's plan as the tallest building you've ever seen in your city. Imagine that is what God is planning to give you. How happy would you be? Yes, that's the same spirit and energy that should be in you right now.

Be happy because His plans are great, beautiful and they are the best. You are a work in progress and very soon, God will unveil to you everything that He has in stock for you. Don't ever give up on God's plan for your life, it may look slow, and it may also look like it's not coming to pass, but you must keep looking at the bigger picture. It is the bigger picture that will make those plans come to a reality earlier.

I believe in you.

DAY 2

IT'S TIME TO AWAKEN FROM YOUR SLUMBER

'*If you faint in the day of adversity, Your strength is small.*' Proverbs 24:10 NKJV.

Recently, I met an old friend that I've known for years. She was looking very good and I had to offer a compliment, 'You look amazing,' I said. 'Oh, thank you. You're too kind,' she replied rather sheepishly.

As we began talking, I realised that the dreamer I used to know in her had disappeared into thin air. Her enthusiasm, joy, and passion for life, the dreams she used to have, all seemed to have been buried. I mean, she used to want to do a Ph.D., host a talk show like Oprah, dance shamelessly as a passionate performer, and even write poetry and wanted to speak about relationships and marriages.

As I gazed into her eyes, I almost asked, 'Where have your dreams gone?'

But I held back. I was careful not to sound like I was judging her. A lot had happened since we used to be quite close and talked about our dreams. Well, maybe not a lot, but she got married and had kids and those dreams appear to have reached the cemetery long before she ever will.

I am reminded of the words of the late Dr Myles Munroe, 'The graveyard is the richest place on the surface of the earth because there you will find the books that were never written or published, ideas that were never put to work, songs that were not sung, and innovations that never saw the light of day.'

Why am I writing this?

I write to those whose dreams have been buried in the sands of life's happenings and busyness. People who have taken on a career turned into a coffin where their glories, potentials, and visions have been buried. They are no longer turned on by their passion. They've gotten so used to mediocrity and the rat race that they no longer see anything else beyond their horizons. Their lives are full of the usual - wake up, get ready for work, get the kids ready, prepare lunch for the day, eat breakfast, and go to work. Come back home, sit on the couch, watch some episodes of their favourite TV series, and off to bed. It's just a cycle.

No more dreams, no more visions, no more purpose. I write to awaken you from this slumber. The purpose of life is to live a life of purpose. And it is dangerous to be alive and not know why or not live for the why for which you were created. The greatest tragedy in life is not death but a life without purpose. You are meant to do something significant; you were not just created to fill some empty spaces. The One who made you made you without any error and He has deposited inside you everything you will ever need to live a purposeful life.

Never let go of those dreams and visions God has been placing on your mind. Let me tell you this secret, you are not just dreaming or seeing visions for seeing sake, God put them there and He didn't put them there for decoration's sake. He put them there so you can bless your generation and generations to come with what He has given to you. There are lots of people who died without their purpose being fulfilled and this is the most tragic thing that can happen to a man.

Sometimes when I talk with people, I wonder how their mind works, and how they think. The only thing some people are thinking about is getting married, having kids, and just living normally. No! That's not God's design and purpose for your life. Though God wants you to get married and live a very good life, life is more than just getting married and giving birth to children. I am not saying getting married and having children is not good. Those things are good because God wants you to get married and have children, but that's not all

God wants you to do. Aside from setting up a family, He also wants you to be purposeful.

God desires that you discover the original reason for which He created you. Hence, you need to wake up from your slumber right now and get to work! Your dreams and vision should not die, you must give expressions to them because that's God's way of expressing Himself through you. Yes, God is pleased when He expresses Himself through humanity. Probably you don't understand that one of the reasons God is giving you those dreams and visions is for expression.

There are countless times that God has expressed Himself through humanity, both in the Scripture and in our contemporary world. God expressed Himself through Moses. Moses used to be an ordinary child, who at the end of the day became an extraordinary man, led the children of Israel out of Egypt, parted the Red Sea, gave water to a whole nation from a rock, brought the Ten Commandments, and so on. Naturally, Moses would not have done those wonders, but God called him for that purpose. What about Joseph, who from the pit, went to Portiphar's house, from there to the prison and then to the palace? All he did to get into the palace was to interpret dreams. God empowered him to do so because he was created for that purpose.

There is a treasure in you waiting for expression, if you don't wake up from your slumber and begin to get things done, you will remain at the lowest level of your life. The amazing part is that God has given you everything you need to fulfill your purpose. If God could call ordinary Moses, a stammerer, and give him the power to do the supernatural, if God could call Joseph and give him the power and wisdom to interpret dreams, then I am certain that God has called you and given you the power to do something.

I challenge you to wake up now and begin to do something with the time, resources, and potential that God has given to you. Don't give up on your purpose, calling, and potential. You have been designed to do something tangible and significant, the power and grace is upon you already, just tap into that grace, and get the ball rolling.

'If you faint in the day of adversity, Your strength is small.' Proverbs 24:10 NKJV.

If you check the above scripture again, you will discover that many people have given up on their dreams and visions because their strength is small. You must develop the wings to fly, don't allow your wings to get weak and weary. If no one is pushing you, you must do everything to push yourself.

Push yourself out of obscurity.

Push yourself out of that darkness.

Push yourself out of the corner of your room.

Push yourself out of your comfort zone.

Now, don't just push yourself, you should rather push yourself beyond your limits because you are unlimited, you are unstoppable. But if you allow those obstacles around you to stop you, then you won't be able to live the life God wanted you to live.

Now is the time to take back your life. Now is the time to dream again or resurrect from those coffins of life. You are not meant to remain at the lowest part of life again, you are designed to be at the top making things happen. Don't rest and don't give up, your life is worth living.

I believe in you.

DAY 3

HOW TO TAKE ACTION FROM WHAT YOU HAVE LEARNT

For years, you have always been hearing that knowledge is power, but I beg to disagree because knowledge is not power, but potential power. The real power is the action you take from what you learn. Acquiring knowledge is not as important as acting upon what you have learnt. I have seen people who read books cover to cover, but they have nothing to show for the knowledge they have been acquiring from the book. Some people attend lectures and seminars and never for once do something about what they have learnt. This is just a waste of time, energy and resources.

Other people would plan and set goals but will never take any action to make their goals a reality. Setting goals is not enough, writing down your plans is not all you need, you also need to do something to propel the movement of what you have set your heart to do. To take action, you need to understand that faith without work is dead.

'For as the body without the spirit is dead, so faith without works is dead also.'

James 2:26 NKJV.

Planning or setting goals without taking action is a mere wish and mere wishes do not come to reality. They often remain in the air without any fruition. Planning without taking action is like having faith without doing work. The two must work together, they are not independent, they are interdependent on one another. So, it means that if you claim to have great faith, then you must be ready to show me your great works. Great faith without great action will equal a great loss. This is one of the greatest mistakes lots of people make. Let me put it another way, great plans or goals without great action will lead to great frustration.

All I am saying, in essence, is that when you learn something, make sure you act upon what you have learnt, don't just sit in the armchair waiting for things to work out automatically. No, life does not work that way. For things to work out, somebody has to work them out. The only person who is responsible for making things work for you is you, so take action now!

Any idea, or vision caught during lectures or teaching are like seeds and they are supposed to be planted so they can sprout forth, if your seeds are not sprouting, then it means all your efforts have come to a waste. If you don't take action, your planning and goals will not bring forth any tangible result. You need to learn how to take inspired action, you can't just be planning or setting goals, without taking corresponding action. Your actions must speak louder than the pen you're using to write your plans and goals.

You should not have any excuse for not going after your goals, the only limitation you have is you, the only person that can stop you is you; you must be up and doing. No excuses for you, those who give excuses for their inaction are those who cannot take responsibility. Don't be like those who are not ready to make a change, rather take charge, take responsibility, and start taking action.

What baffles me most about people is that they are waiting for the right time and season before they can start doing something. No, great people don't grow that way, great people start with what they have and from where they are. Start from where you are, start with the little resources on your hands right now. You don't need to have all the money in the world before you can start action. Always know that the more you waste time, the more you waste away. Start now, and grow tomorrow, the journey to greatness will start with one small and little but giant. Those who do great things are those who do it afraid, they jump into the river without knowing how to swim, you must jump as well, if you jump, what will make you swim will come upon you.

I want to help you with four keys to help you take advantage of anything you learn:

1. Use the ACT principle:

A - Apply | What can you apply right now?

This helps you to get into action mode right away. Anything you don't use, you lose. I love this popular saying, 'Wisdom is the right application of knowledge.' To apply something is to act upon something. There won't be an application without an action, that is why it is called application which means apply and action. I challenge you to get into action mode right now, don't even wait till tomorrow before you take action.

C - Change | What will you change right now?

This question helps you to reflect on what you are currently doing that is probably not working and then you can change it. Change is constant, things change, places change, people change, and so on. You should change too because you can't be doing things the way you have been doing them and expect things to change or work automatically. You must be ready to adapt to changes, don't assume things will automatically change by themselves. People who reinvent and re-innovate don't wait for circumstances to change on their own, they rather make the changes happen. They act upon what they know. Those who are waiting for things to change are those not ready to make things happen. One of Newton's laws of motion states that all bodies will continue to be in a state of rest or uniform motion unless acted upon by an external force.

You are the external force that will act upon your body, life, and circumstances around you. I challenge you to start making the change at the moment.

T - Teach/Tell | What can you teach from what you learnt?

When you teach what you know, you can never forget it. So, share what you know. It's a powerful tool to help you be accountable and take action. Teaching what you know will make you a master of that particular thing. Don't dare make the mistake of keeping what you know to yourself, teach others, organise classes, or create a WhatsApp or Telegram group; it may be a group of five, ten, or twenty people, the goal is to teach people what you have learnt and know because one of the secrets of high flyers is that they teach other people what they know because they understand the power of repetition. The more you repeatedly tell others what you understand about a particular subject or course, the more you will know and understand that subject.

2. **Ask yourself: What is the simple or smallest thing I got from what I learnt that I can start doing daily?**

So, after studying or learning something, make sure you make it a habit to always look at your notes and see what small things you can start doing daily or consistently. You must not be without doing something. For instance, if you have learnt how to speak publicly, you must not wait till you get thousands of crowds before you start speaking, rather start by speaking to yourself. David did not start by confronting Goliath, he started by confronting lions in the forest. David did not start by being the king of Israel, he started by being the king of wild animals in the forest. Start doing something right now from where you are. If you don't start anything, you will not get anywhere. That's the truth!

Then, when you have started, make sure you are consistent with what you have started. Consistency may not be an easy task to do, but you must be consistent. It may be about being consistent with your brand. It may be hunting for coaching or shopping for your greatness, it could be learning daily. Make sure you are consistent about doing something. Make sure an action point is there for you to do daily and consistently.

Remember, persistence helps you get it but consistency helps you keep it.

3. Be Accountable: Find someone you will be sharing what you are learning with.

Until you have someone/platform where you are constantly sharing all that you're learning, you will not feel you are growing. Growth is powerful when you keep sharing what you are learning. Accountability aids growth. If you are not accountable to someone, you will not have reasons to continue doing what you are doing. Be accountable, get a responsible person or people, and begin to give an account to them. The secret of accountability is that it helps you to remain consistent about what you are doing, it also helps you know whether you are doing well, improving or not.

I believe in you.

DAY 4

IS YOUR FUSE BLOWN?

Some years ago, in one of our previous houses, one day we noticed our kitchen didn't have electricity whereas other parts of the house had it.

Our electric cooker was not working, the toaster, hot water kettle, everything in the kitchen that used electricity just would not work.

However, we were able to watch TV in the living room, and the lights in the bedroom appeared okay.

I tried all I could to troubleshoot the issue but nothing changed until we called an electrician who pointed out that the kitchen had a fuse in the main electrical box.

The fuse was the source of all the electricity that goes into the kitchen. The fuse blew, so no electricity could flow from it.

Why am I sharing this with you?

Just like none of the appliances in the kitchen could work because their source blew, in the same way, none of us can function without connection to God our Father. God is our source - the electricity, and the fuse is our heart.

Whether we are big or small, it's the connection to God, our Father, that makes us useful and powerful. What makes a difference between those making godly and kingdom exploits is God, He is our source and the moment we attach ourselves to Him, we will remain connected and nothing on earth will blow us out.

If you don't want to blow out and away, you must make God your source and remain connected to Him. You, being in connection with God will make a big difference in your life. We are mortal humans and we can't do anything without the immortal God. He created us, He understands our frame, He knows the kind of stuff we are made up of and He just wants us to remain connected with Him because He knows we are feeble creatures capable of breaking at any slight instance.

Jesus summed this up nicely when He said, '*I can do nothing on my own. I judge as God tells me. Therefore, my judgment is just, because I carry out the will of the one who sent me, not my own will.*' - *John 5:30 NLT*.

Your connection with God is as important as the breath you take in daily. You must daily fix yourself to Him, there should be no day that you should detach yourself from Him, otherwise, you may blow away. You can do nothing if you detach yourself from Him. For you to fulfill your purpose and carry out God's calling on your life, you must stay connected to God, and you must ensure your fuse is not blown.

A lot of people, even many Christians, want to do life and purpose without involving God, the implication of that is that you will never have the real life in doing what you are doing.

'In Him was life, and the life was the light of men.' John 1:4 NKJV.

In God was life, so how do you intend to do life without the life Himself? There is nothing you can do without Him in you and you in Him. If you are passionate about living a good and purposeful life, you must remain in Him. The more you live in God, the more you know and understand the depth of life.

Life in God is like a light constantly moving or flowing in a cable. Without the flow of electric current in a cable, there won't be a supply of electricity and as a result, there won't be a supply of light. That's exactly how most people are living their lives today. The truth is that many people are living their lives without God in them. You see, God is a constant flowing divine current that needs the fuse of your life to be intact for all the appliances of your life to be in order.

If you want your life to be in order, you must also be in good order with God. Don't ever allow busy schedules and activities to get you distracted from connecting to God. Don't be clouded with your loads of cares, they will only get you disconnected from God and when you get disconnected, you might blow away.

Hence, for you not to blow away, you must guard your fuse (your heart) jealously. Here is what the Bible says about guarding your heart: *'Above all else, guard your heart, for everything you do flows from it.'* - Proverbs 4:23 NIV.

Your heart is like the engine room of your life, if you don't guard it well and jealously, you may lose current, disconnect from God, and blow away. Guard your heart with everything you have, if your heart stays connected with God, then nothing will move you away from God, don't you know that out of your heart flows everything - both good and evil? If you allow your heart to get stuck with God, then only the good will be permitted to flow out of your life. If you are disconnected from God, negative thinking and occurrences will flow out of your life, because you are disconnected from your source!

If you are going to effectively fulfill your life's purpose, you must learn to guard your heart. The truth is God consistently communicates with you through your heart, so He needs your heart to be right always. If your heart is right, everything about your life will be right. Check your heart today, and make sure God is still flowing through it to you and all areas of your life.

I believe in you.

DAY 5
SOMETIMES YOU WIN, SOMETIMES YOU LEARN

My kids were playing chess with each other the other day and I overheard the younger one say to his brother, 'Sometimes you win, sometimes you learn.'

I can't recollect who won or lost the game but that phrase gladdened my heart. It gladdened my heart because we didn't start with that phrase but I am glad they got it.

We used to tell them, 'Sometimes you win, sometimes you lose,' until one day when I got an epiphany and I told my wife that we had to change that statement.

We did! We changed it to 'Sometimes you win, sometimes you learn.'

We have been intentional in teaching them that there is nothing called failure. In life, you learn from the things that do not work out, you also gain from your losses. Losing is an opportunity to reflect on their learnings and opportunities.

Henry Ford said it better, 'Failure is simply an opportunity to begin again, this time more intelligently.'

You are not a failure because your plans didn't later work out, you are not a failure because you couldn't execute that project you are not even a failure because you lost thousands of dollars on a business deal that didn't later work out well, you are not a failure because you had a divorce and your life seems shattered and life itself seems unreal and unfair.

On some occasions, some of the horrible things that happen to us come to teach us lessons of life. God is so gracious that He knows everything about us and He planned how our life circumstances and events would go. So when it looks like we fail, fall, or falter, it is not so because God will always work everything out for our good. Sometimes, you might be going through those challenges so you can learn and be built up.

Sometimes, life can be funny, things we didn't plan for will come up and we will just have to face them. The truth is that you can't always have the good balls to yourself, bad ones would mix up with the good ones. In other words, you won't always have good and pleasant experiences, some horrible ones may creep in at a point in your life, but you must be deliberate about learning your lessons from those circumstances.

You can't always win. That's the bitter truth, but you can always learn. You can never stop learning, your whole life depends on it. So, when it seems you failed at something, don't look at it from the standpoint of failure, look at it from the standpoint of learning. You are learning whenever you have little or big setbacks, don't lose your mind over what didn't work out, rather stay strong.

You thought failure was your end, or that failure was a loss, God said I should tell you that you're wrong. Not all losses take away something from you, many of them have added things to you. You might not see what your losses added to you, but definitely, they added an unseen growth. You are always drawing closer to your desired results when you fail and learn something because you have learnt new lessons. If only you will be calm enough to learn from your failure, then your life will begin to move on a smoother path.

Stop focusing on failures, focus on learning, and stop focusing on what you are losing, rather start focusing on the experiences you are gaining. I am glad to inform you that God is much more interested in your growth than in your fall. He is more interested in your gain than in your pains, that's why when you fail, He is not focusing on those failures, even when you go through pains, He focuses on what you will later gain. Your problem is that you keep focusing on the pain instead of on the gain. Focus on the big picture, not on the little ditch you are falling into.

Joseph focused on the big picture, not on the pains he was going through. He sure had a dream of being a king, he had a dream of becoming a great man, and he sure had a dream that people would bow to him. Joseph never planned for the day he would be thrown in the pit, he never planned for the day he would be a slave in a strange land. He never planned that he would ever go to prison. He went through life and life went through him, Joseph never gave up on what he saw, he was rather learning through his pains. Can you just be like Joseph who in spite of his challenges refused to give up, refused to count himself as a failure, but rather fought until he later got to the palace as a prime minister?

There is a place you are going, that's why you are going through all you are going through right now. Your pains are not meant to land you into shame, they are rather meant to get you into gains. If Joseph did not land in shame, then I'm sure you won't land in shame. Focus on learning, focus on gains, and focus on getting a big deal out of all you are presently going through. Can I shock you? There are gains for you in every pain. There is a lesson in every loss. This is why you must continue to work on the big picture you have seen about the future. Obstacles will come, but they won't overwhelm you if you are strong enough to fight to the end like Joseph.

No wonder the Bible says, *'And we know that all things work together for good to those who love God, to those who are the called according to His purpose.'[Romans 8:28 NKJV]*

I strongly understand the above scripture, nothing is happening in your life right now for the sake of happening, there are specific reasons why some situations present themselves to you and you just have to embrace them, rather than fighting against them.

Meanwhile, I want to encourage you to be purposeful. A man of purpose is a man on a mission, and when you are on a mission, obstacles will always come out looking for you, but when you are living a life of purpose, you will never lose even if life seems hard, tough, and difficult. You will always win in the end.

Never forget those words, 'Sometimes you win, sometimes you learn.'

I believe in you.

DAY 6
LESSONS ABOUT GROWTH

Recently, my wife told me about a coaching programme she would like to pay for. The programme was quite expensive and she asked what I thought about her decision to take the programme.

I asked for the details of the programme and she explained the value she would get from it. Without hesitation, I asked her to go ahead.

Over the last few years, I have learnt two valuable lessons about growth:

1. When it comes to your personal growth, stop thinking price, start thinking value!
2. Growth will cost you.

Growth will demand that something leaves your hand, but then, know for sure that when something leaves your hand, something will come into your heart. You will be built and upgraded.

Free is a trap; a trap that keeps you in your comfort zone. Many people are falling into the trap of free seminars, free training, free mentorship, and so on. Many don't want to pay for training, that's why they are not also growing. Your growth in life depends solely on how much you are willing to pay for the growth. If you are not ready to sacrifice and pay for your growth, you will never experience growth. If you want to reach your potential in life, you must be willing to sacrifice. Sacrifice may cost you a whole lot, but you must be willing to pay it.

The truth is that no matter how impactful a training might be if you don't subscribe to it by paying, you will never maximise it to your advantage. That's why people are not growing. The cost of growth is expensive, you will get better for what you sacrifice for. Paying for growth is not a waste, it is worth it. No amount is too much to get wisdom. Wisdom is essential and you just do everything in your capacity to get it.

'Wisdom is the principal thing; Therefore get wisdom. And in all your getting, get understanding.'

Proverbs 4:7 NKJV.

Wisdom may be costly but do all you can to get it because it is the principal thing. It is the principal thing because wisdom is what you cannot live or do without and one of the ways by which you can get it is by paying for it. Paying to get wisdom gives you real value. Value is not easy to get, it is quite expensive. Solomon understood the value of wisdom. He knew that to get it, you must pay or sacrifice something for it, so he advised that it is the principal thing, therefore it must be gotten. In his undertone, I can hear him screaming, 'It may be costly, but get it by all means!'

Information is free but transformation will cost you something.

John Maxwell said, 'When you see people who are not growing, you would notice it is often down to the price they have to pay to grow.' Well, most people do think it's too expensive. Nothing is too expensive if it has to do with growth matters. The amazing part is that most people prefer to buy the latest iPhone, expensive and latest designers than to pay for what will give them value. Let me tell you something, you are the sole proprietor of your destiny after God and it is quite unfortunate that God will never come down to do for you what He knows you can do for yourself.

God won't come down to pay or register you for a training, seminar, or mentorship programme. You must be responsible for it; you must be intentional about it. Those who desire to grow are those who desire to add value to their lives. Great values are gotten and grabbed not by freebies. People rather sacrifice for it. Meanwhile, don't also make the mistake of thinking things will naturally or automatically get better when you are not putting in the right effort. No, things don't get better like that, things are worked out. If you don't work things out, you will always remain at the lowest level of your life.

I will also challenge you to move out of your comfort zone. Your comfort zone may be one of your greatest enemies of growth. If you are comfortable with a particular level for a long period, then it means you are operating in mediocrity and you are not ready for a change. Change is the only constant thing, and for change to happen, there is a price to pay. Many people are stuck in their comfort zone because they are not ready to pay the price to leave that zone. Living in a comfort zone is like living in a trap, and if care is not well taken, you will never get out of that trap.

You must do anything and everything possible to get out of your comfort zone, you must not stay there again. God told the Israelites to get out of their comfort zone too. Yes, they were indeed eating free food, getting free water, living in free houses, and doing everything for free in their comfort zone, yet God told them to evacuate. God knew that if they remained in their comfort zone, they wouldn't occupy the land He had promised them and if they wouldn't occupy the land, His promises for them wouldn't be fulfilled.

The truth is that God wants you to leave the place you are at the moment. He wants you to go out and learn something new. He wants you to be released from the bondage of your comfort zone so you can occupy more spaces in the Promised Land you are going to.

God is interested in your growth. In fact, He would have taken you to the next phase of that ministry, business, career, and other things by now, but your unwillingness to pay a price for the next phase is keeping you down. You are not ready to pay the price and sacrifice financially, time-wise, in service, accountability, and consistency and that's why you have not been moving.

Many are not willing to move out of their comfort zone, they would rather stay where they are comfortable and secure not realising their value is beyond their comfort zone. When God wants to change your life, He shows you the price you must pay for it.

Are you willing to pay the price for your growth?

I believe in you.

DAY 7

BE A PERSON OF VALUE

I was part of a meeting my colleague invited me to recently and after about an hour into the meeting, I started to ask myself the following questions:

1. Am I adding value to anyone here?
2. Is this going to help my purpose or future?
3. Is this part of my job description and what I'm being paid to do?

I realised the answers to those questions were negative. At that time, I realised I was wasting time and was only there to please my colleague. I immediately excused myself and off I went.

Why am I sharing this with you?

1. **Never do anything for the sake of just pleasing people.**

If it doesn't serve God's purpose for your life or add value to people's lives, you should not be found there.

You are a person of value, and your time is valuable. Don't waste it! A lot of people don't understand this, they don't even know how to say, 'No!' You are valueless if you are frequently found in a place where your purpose will not be serviced. In life, it's either you are servicing someone, or someone is servicing you. If none of the two is happening, then you don't value your time. Time is important, it is one of the greatest gifts God gave to humanity in a measure. The rich and the poor have the same measure of time, the successful and the failures also have the same measure of time. If you truly want to be a person of value, you must be a person who has high regard for time. If you don't have regard for your time, you won't live a productive life.

Hence, for you to be productive, you must also be ready to be valuable. You should not even make the mistake of thinking that it is only when you please people that you will be valuable. As I noted earlier, if it's not adding to your life, then you are in for a shock. The only person you are not permitted to say, 'No' to is God. If God is asking you to do something, go somewhere, or give something out, you dare not say, 'No' to Him. This is because there is nothing God will ask you to do that will not add value to your life in the end. If you are working for a company, all that the company wants from you is value. If your availability is not giving value to that company, they will sack you and stop you from working for them.

The truth is, you can't do without being a man or woman of value. Even if you are married to a spouse, you are in that marital relationship to consistently give value. You can't be taking and taking from the other person, without giving back. The essence of every relationship is to give value at the end. If your existence is not adding something tangible to another person's life, then that person may cease to exist in your life, even if the person is your spouse. One of the reasons divorces are at a high rate these days is that a lot of people have this wrong mindset about marriage; they only want to get married to get, buy with the other party's money, and enjoy their lives. Most people don't understand what it means to be a person of value. You can't be taking all the time without giving something, the other person will get tired of you.

All I'm telling you right now is to be a person of value. If you don't become a person of value, people will get tired of you. In fact, the world won't pay attention to you.

People are paying so much attention to some of these social media content creators and comedians because they are giving value to people. They are dishing out educational, informative, and funny content. People pay attention to them because they have what they can offer that any other person could not probably offer. A lot of people can waste their data subscriptions to watch a 30-minute-long comedy. All they want to derive is pleasure and happiness. Meanwhile, as they see these contents on social media with their data subscriptions, the content creator is getting richer. They are getting richer because they are frequently dishing out content.

Value giving is the gateway to wealth, if you can know how to be a person of value and offer value as a product or service, you will become a sought-after person. The richest man in Nigeria right now is wealthy not because he is handsome, especially brilliant, or highly intelligent. No, he is just valuable. He knows and understands the needs of the people and he offers such needs to them. What can you also offer to people?

Do you know that people will not pay you because you are handsome, they won't pay you because you are tall. In fact, they won't pay you because you are educated and you have your certificate; they will only pay you because of your ability to deliver something valuable.

2. The awareness of your purpose sets your priorities in life.

Even though you can do all things through Christ who strengthens you, it doesn't mean you have to do all things. One of the most important things in life is to note that even though all things are lawful for you, not all of them are beneficial. You can't be all things to all men, setting your priorities will help you recognise opportunities easier, you will understand that it is not all the opportunities that present themselves to you that you will accept. You should not be available to do everything, but you should be available to do everything that goes in line with your purposes. Don't make the mistake of doing Jack of all trades, it will take you nowhere. You are responsible for choosing what to go for and what not to go for. Focus on what matters to you, stop poke-nosing into what everyone is doing, focus on yourself, and focus on your job.

The secret to setting priorities is to identify your purpose. The awareness of your purpose will set your life in order, you will know what's important and what's not important to you. Be on a mission, be sold out to fulfilling God's purpose for your life. You can't choose to be at every place at all times. An awareness of your purpose will set your life on track, make you handle responsibilities, and make you know what priorities you should focus on.

'*Making the most of your time because the days are evil.*'
Ephesians 5:16 NASB.

Make the most of your time, be sold out, and set priorities for yourself. The awareness of God's purpose for your life helps you to differentiate the essential from the non-essential.

The demand you place on your abilities and your time has to be following your purpose. Life is too short and you don't have eternity to do what you were created to do, so you must be wise in this regard.

I believe in you.

DAY 8

TIME WAS GIVEN FOR PURPOSE

Some years ago, I set an examination for some of my students and I happened to be the invigilator as well. On the day of the exam, as usual, some students were prepared and ready, and some were not. I remember when it was just about 10 minutes to the end of the paper, one of the students called me and said, 'Dr Samuel, can you extend the time? The time you have given is not enough?'

I couldn't help but laugh at his request. It was funny to me because before he made his request, seven students had submitted. In other words, 7 out of 25 students had completed their work way ahead of time, whereas this student was there saying the time allotted was not enough at 10 minutes to go.

Why am I sharing this with you?

Like that examination, life is an assignment, and there is a time allotted. No matter how much we desire to live long, all of us have our lifetime ordained by God.

How do I know this? Hear this, ***'You have decided the length of our lives. You know how many months we will live, and we are not given a minute longer.'*** *Job 14:5 NLT.*

This means whatever you were born to do, you don't have eternity or forever to do it.

Stop wasting time and blaming God when you come to the end of your life, saying the time He gave you was not enough. As I noted in the previous chapter, the same measure of time was given to both the rich and the poor and the rich are rich because they maximise the time that was allotted to them. You don't have a choice but to maximise the time that is allotted to you by God because you will not always have the time on your side. You are responsible for making the most of your time. If you don't know how to make use of your time, then there will be those who will know how to waste it.

I have seen other people who are used to fulfilling other people's purposes because they have no clue about how they can maximise their own time. If you know how to take control of your time, you will also know how to take control of your life. If you meet highly productive people, you will notice something about them, they don't joke with their time. One minute out of their time means a lot and they cherish that one minute. The case is rather different for unproductive people, they can waste a whole hour on an unproductive event. I have seen men who spent more than two hours of their time in a football viewing center. This is bad and a waste of resources.

I am not against love for sport and soccer, but there must be time for everything. If you don't know how to live a purposeful life, other events will take up your time on your behalf. You are responsible for making the most of your time and to make the most of your time, you must spend it on purpose.

Everyone is called to do and fulfill their purpose. In this life, it's either you are fulfilling your purpose or you're not fulfilling your purpose. If you are living a purposeful life, then it means your life is counting, if you are not living a purposeful life, then it means you have to reschedule and reshuffle your life. You must be on an assignment, it's a must! You must not be redundant, you just be purposeful. The time God gave you is not meant for frivolous activities, it is meant for productive activities.

Time was given for purpose.

The Bible says, **'To everything there is a season, A time for every purpose under heaven.'** Ecclesiastes 3:1 NKJV.

The above verse suggests that there is a time at which an event happens in life is significant. What may be helpful and right at one moment may be wrong at another moment. If you grasp this understanding, you will know that purpose fulfilling has timing. There is a specific time allotted for a specific purpose to be achieved in your life.

Therefore, it is dangerous to be given time and not know why.

Don't be an unserious student. Find your purpose today and begin to live a purposeful life. God is counting on you and generations await the manifestation of God's gifts and His glory through you.

The surest way to be a victim of time is to waste it or be ignorant of it.

Don't be a victim. Be purposeful with your time. Time is a precious commodity that you must use wisely. It is your most valuable resource, and you must make the most of every moment. To live with the consciousness of purpose means you remember the 'Why' of your life. Many people don't understand the 'Why' of their lives, and that's why they can't find better activities to use their time for.

Time is an important part of our lives. It gives order and priorities to our days and it allows us to set our schedules right. But the tragic part is that your schedules have no power in themselves unless they are planned with your purpose in mind. It would be useless and a waste of energy to keep track of your time if there is no end toward which you are moving.

I believe in you.

DAY 9
KNOWLEDGE AUDIT

Let me share one of my secrets with you real quick.

One of the things I do often that helps me fulfill my purpose effectively is what I call a knowledge audit.

I sit in a very quiet place and I look at my goals. I take each goal one by one and ask myself,

'What do I need to know/learn to be able to achieve each of my goals?' I always do this with my journal and pen so I can write out the ideas that come to mind.

I then would identify the coaching, workshops, seminars, and YouTube videos that I need to access to help me learn those things.

In some of those sessions, I draft questions I would ask my mentors at our next meeting.

This is me being intentional about my purpose and life. You see, doing this frequently will enable you to be accountable to yourself. In this regard, accountability will bring you progress and productivity.

For anyone that would fulfill their purpose, you have to do your knowledge audit regularly. Stop pampering yourself, and audit yourself, this will enable you to know whether you are doing well or not.

One of the goals of knowledge audit is to make you indicate the progress in your life, and it is to be properly and carefully carried out. Knowledge audit will enhance growth, and exposure and will enable you to know what and what not to do at a certain time. You should not make the mistake of living your life for a whole two or three months without personal assessment. It helps a lot, it makes you generate more ideas, gives you insight into your progress, and gives you ideas about how you can set or draw out your personal growth agenda.

To do a knowledge audit, you need to be intentional about it. Go to a place of solitude, sit alone, pick a pen and a pad, and begin to ask yourself serious questions. Meanwhile, asking yourself serious questions is not enough to make any progress. As you are asking yourself serious and honest questions, you must also give serious and honest answers to those questions. Because it is your answers to the questions you asked that will give you ideas about how you can move from where you are at the moment to where you ought to be.

Ask yourself:

What do I need to know?

What do I need to learn?

What questions do I need to ask?

Who are the people I need to meet?

What conference do I need to attend?

What workshop or seminar will help me learn these things?

What course do I need to take?

What podcast do I need to start listening to?

The answer to some of these questions will cost you something - your time, your money, your comfort zone, and even relationships.

You must be ready. You must make a plan to pay that price.

So, when next are you doing your own audit?

I believe in you.

DAY 10
YOUR PURPOSE IS VALID

I saw something in the Bible recently that touched me.

Let me share it with you because I know it will help you too.

I was studying Matthew chapter 3, where Jesus came to John the Baptist for Him to be baptized. Before Jesus arrived at the scene, John had been telling people about Jesus saying,

'I baptize with water those who repent of their sins and turn to God. But someone is coming soon who is greater than I am—so much greater that I'm not worthy even to be his slave and carry his sandals. He will baptize you with the Holy Spirit and with fire.' Matthew 3:11 NLT.

When Jesus got to the river and saw John, he asked to be baptized.

John recognised him and said, 'I am the one who needs to be baptized by you so why are you coming to me?'

Jesus' answer is worth studying for months. He said, '***...It should be done, for we must carry out all that God requires...' Matthew 3:15 NLT.***

Jesus was simply saying, 'This is out of our hands, it has been ordained for you to baptise me. It's your purpose and I can't carry out my purpose if you don't do yours.'

Wow! Did you catch that?

No one's purpose is insignificant.

Let me say that again, your purpose is very valid. Your purpose is very significant and crucial. Just as no one is useless in life, so there is no useless purpose. Even if you think your purpose is insignificant, it has a lot to do for people and this is why you must not despise the little assignment God has given to you to fulfil. John the Baptist was sent with the purpose of preparing the way for the Lord. To humans, this purpose is unimportant and may seem to have no significance. But to God, it is important.

You may be going through a season right now where you think your purpose has no significance, it may look like people are not taking cognizance of what you are doing, and it may even look like people are rejecting you at the moment, but you must look past people's rejection and move towards your God-given mandate. Your purpose is valid. John the Baptist was sent as the one who would prepare the way for the Lord, it is significant. Let me tell you something, even if your purpose is to clean chairs in church, it is significant and you must do it wholeheartedly and faithfully too.

Don't make the mistake of pursuing or fulfilling another person's purpose. Everyone's purpose is designed and peculiar to them, your purpose is also peculiar to you and you must be serious about it. Another thing you need to note is that if no one is clapping for you for what you are doing, always know that heaven is clapping for you.

Understand this truth and be set free - No one's purpose is better than yours. Don't make the mistake of that man who went to hide his talent because his master gave him only one talent. The servant thought that his talent was insignificant, so he went to bury it. At the end of the day, what he buried and refused to use was given to another person who worked and gained extra. This is the secret, if you take your purpose with seriousness and you are always on a mission to fulfill it, more would be given to you. The very one that you think is invalid and insignificant, be faithful to it. The more faithful you are to it, the more purpose you will receive to fulfill.

Don't despise what God has given to you, rather embrace it and be on a mission with it. That small thing will bring the big deal out of your life. From today, never look down on your purpose, or yourself or think your life does not count.

What God requires of you is the source of your significance and influence.

When you see people who appear greater and bigger than you, don't be intimidated. Those people also started from a place and they are where they are today because they see what they do as significant. If only you can be consistent with what God has given to you or called you to do, then you will also go far in life. Don't be surprised that most times, what makes great men great are things that have no significance, things people don't consider to be great, things people look away from. You are not in the position to rate what you are called to fulfill, only God is in that position. So, even if you think what you are called to do is insignificant or small, you must be on a mission to fulfill it.

You need to realise that those who are doing greater works stay within the confines of their calling, they are doing their purpose and you just need to find yours and begin to live in it. We all are a part of God's big plan. We need each other to bring God's kingdom down on earth.

Don't let anyone look down on you, but more importantly, don't look down on yourself. You matter a lot, and if you don't matter, God would not have created you in the first place.

Say to yourself, 'I matter! My purpose is valid.'

Say it loud and let the devil hear you!

Hallelujah! I feel like screaming! Do you feel me?

I believe in you.

DAY 11

BEGIN TODAY! START NOW!

Do you know that 80% of people on their deathbeds wish they had done more with their lives?

They wish they could have done more, loved more, became more, given more, and impacted more people. As soon as it's announced to them that they are about to die, they start to regret not doing enough with their lives.

Without being unnecessarily morbid, I want to challenge you today, please don't wait till you're about to die before you start doing more with your life.

Don't wait till when it's a few days to go and then you start impacting your world and trying to make a mark, it would have been late by then.

Begin today! Start now!

Now is the accepted time, today is the day of salvation.

Even if you are still on the journey of purpose discovery, begin to do something with your gifts and talents. Start small. You don't have to be great to start but you have to start to be great.

Start adding value to people every single day. No matter how small you may think you are, there will be something you can do better than someone out there. You may be able to sing, dance, draw, make snacks, and drive. Nothing is insignificant before God. There is nothing God cannot use to make your life up, there is nothing God can't use to lift and bless people. Your singing can bless people. In fact, the internet and social media have made everything easier, you don't even need to book a studio session before you can sing for the world to hear you out. Start with recording on your small phone, do a video of yourself singing, put it on social media, and let people see it, someone can be blessed through it.

Are you talented at drawing? Then start drawing today! Make your drawing and put it on social media. The truth is that the advent of social media has made more people activate the power of their purposes. There is no doubt that this same social media has caused more havoc to people than good. But all you have to do with it is to be smarter! Make use of social media to your advantage. Stop waiting for things and circumstances to get better and look rosy before you start dishing out what God has blessed you with. Even in that small room of yours, you can start something!

Are you called into the ministry? Then start it, stop waiting for the time you will have all the money to rent a big space before you can start. Start now, start in your small room. Even if it's not well organised, just take the bold step and start. Nothing is stopping you from starting somewhere, you are the person stopping yourself from starting what God has called you to start. The truth is, you can't always have everything figured out, there will always be reasons why you should not start, but you must look beyond those reasons and start something worthwhile.

Time is not on your side, life is too short to waste it. The more you waste time, the more you waste your life, and the more you waste your life, the more you waste away. Stop giving excuses, you should rather be in charge and start something. Begin today, start now, you are worth more than just waiting for the right time because no matter how long you wait, the right time can never come, you will just keep waiting, hoping, and praying.

You need to make a decision today; you need to decide that you will not die ordinary. The ball is in your court, no one can decide on your behalf, you are in the best position to decide for yourself what you will do with your life right now. Is it not better to start now than to keep postponing the starting time?

Decide that you will live fully and die empty; that you will not add to the wealth of the grave.

YOUR PURPOSE WILL COST YOU EVERYTHING!

The world is waiting for your manifestation and God is counting on you.

DAY 12
YOUR PURPOSE WILL COST YOU EVERYTHING

Your purpose will cost all that you have because it is a work of sacrifice. I want that to sink in for a minute.

Now, let's move, let me explain.

You see, when Jesus called His first disciples, Peter and his brother, Andrew, all He said to them was, '*...Follow me and I will make you fishers of men.*' Matthew 4:19 NKJV.

That was all they heard, and all they needed to hear.

Guess what? The Bible recorded,
'*They immediately left their nets and followed Him.*'
Matthew 4:20 NKJV.

The word 'immediately' there is so powerful. One of the things God has been showing me lately is that obedience is a journey but it starts with an immediate step. What I'm saying in essence is that you must also leave all that you are doing to follow God. If you cannot leave all to follow God, then you are not ready to live a purposeful life. Those who live a purposeful life are those who are completely sold out for God. You cannot be fully purposeful if you're not completely sold out for God.

Anyone you see out there who does greater works for God are those who have completely sold themselves out for God. I'm talking about those who do exploits for the kingdom of God. This is what God wants you to do as well, to be used greatly in His kingdom. Don't get this wrong, you don't need to be a pastor on a pulpit before you can do great exploits for God.

A lot of people have this misconception about working in God's kingdom, people think until they start preaching on the pulpit, they won't fulfill the mandate of God for their lives. You can be a tech person and still be on a full-time mission fulfilling God's purposes for your life. You can be a university lecturer and still be useful in God's kingdom. What's important to you is to make sure you are following just as His disciples left everything to follow Him.

Following God starts with faith. Believing without seeing. Acting immediately as you're told. God loves people who obey Him without questioning Him. Do you know that this was how Father Abraham became accepted to God? God told him to leave his father's country for a strange land he had never been to. Without any questioning, Abraham left all, by faith, and followed God's leading.

To fulfill the purpose of God for your life, you must be willing to follow God's leading, you must be willing to leave everything, you must be willing to sell yourself out completely for God, and you must be willing to go the extra mile for Him.

The secret is: God won't reveal the whole plan to you, He won't reveal everything to you, He just wants you to follow His leadings, He wants you to obey. Most times, God will only show you where He is taking you; He won't reveal the whole picture, especially how you will get there. He will always hide the processes from you just as He did to Abraham. He will often leave the details of how you will get there out but you must still trust Him by leaving everything else to obey Him.

Peter left his nets to follow Jesus. Do you know the implication of that? He said 'goodbye' to his long-time profession. He completely forsook his daily business for the sake of Jesus. That sounds impossible and a natural man will never do that. Only a spiritual man with a discerning spirit will set out on that kind of assignment.

I have a question for you today, what are your own 'nets' today? What is that thing you are not willing to leave to pursue your purpose?

For some of you, it's the security of the rat race of your career. For some, it's the praise and opinions of people about them. For some, it's the pursuit of wealth and affluence. For others, it's the need to belong to a group of people.

Listen, purpose will cost you your nets, and if you are going to live a fulfilled and successful life in God's account, you must be willing to let go of your nets today.

You know your nets. You may pretend as if you don't but you do, so cast them off right now for the sake of purpose and fulfillment. God has been speaking to you all along. You know what's holding you back.

Don't let them hold you back anymore!

I believe in you.

DAY 13

SUCCESS LEAVES CLUES

One of the things that have helped me a lot in life is those I surround myself with. Some years ago, I surrounded myself with people who had no idea about their purpose in life.

So, none of our discussions had anything to do with purpose, making an impact, or pursuing the kingdom of God.

We were always talking about becoming rich or making more money, getting a better/bigger job, and buying properties.

Now, my circle has changed. My friends consist of people who want to fulfill their purpose, win souls, and pursue God's kingdom. We have these in common and are willing to achieve them together. As a result, my motivation and drive for life have gotten better and I live every day charged up to fulfill my purpose.

Why am I sharing this with you?

If you want to do great things in life, you must surround yourself with others who are doing great things. Your circles of friends and relationships matter a lot, if you roll and move with four nonentities, then you didn't count very well because you guys are five, you complete the number. A friend to a nonentity is a nonentity himself, that's just the bitter truth. If you don't move with people who are going somewhere, you will also end up nowhere.

It is also important for you to surround yourself with those who are motivated and hopeful about their future. If not, the future will look like a mirage to you, it will be a mere dream that can never come to a reality. Be intentional about your life and be intentional about your choice of friends and relationships because your relationship defines who you are as a person.

'He who walks with wise men will be wise, But the companion of fools will be destroyed.' Proverbs 13:20 NKJV.

The above scripture needs no further explanation, you will, at the end of the day, be the direct replica of the relationships you are keeping around yourself. You must keep good company. Keeping the right company will keep your life in shape, and make you futuristic. Because when you move and roll with people who often talk and discuss the future, the future will interest you, will look real to you, and will make you have solid plans for the future. The people you constantly talk to and see will affect the direction of your life, whether you like it or not. What you are beholding consistently is what you will eventually become.

The language you speak daily, you will soon become fluent at it. If it's the language of failure, you will soon be speaking fluent failure. If it's the language of success, you will soon become fluent in it. I strongly advise people not to keep company with a person who has frequent records of failures. Well, I understand that life is in phases, an individual may be having some setbacks at the moment, but that's not what I'm talking about because it won't stay like that forever. But when you have examined someone's life, especially his past and present and you can't notice any traces of success, please run for your dear future's sake.

When you surround yourself with great people, you either start to feel like you're not doing enough, your life is wasting away, or that you could do more. Trust me, those are great feelings, as long as they prompt you to action and not depression. It is healthy to get motivated by another person's success. If you have been feeling this way, now is the time to swing to action. Don't be ashamed to ask that friend of yours, who is an achiever, the secret to their success. When you ask them, please don't just be curious, be determined to apply whatever secrets they share with you.

Keeping relationships with people who frequently have a taste of success will push you to do more with your life and for others. Your movement in life depends solely on those you have chosen to be within your circle. You can't be with a person who is not seeing beyond his locality while you have the dream of going global. To go global and take the world, you must also move with the person seeing what you are seeing and going where you are going.

The truth is that success leaves clues. If you want to be successful, learn what successful people are doing, learn the principles, and begin to live by them. There is no way you will move with the blessed and not be blessed. Abraham was a blessed man, anyone who became the friend of Abraham at that time will eventually become blessed too because success and blessings are like a magnet, they attract anyone that is around them.

If you truly desire to be successful, then start checking out for those who have the results you are seeking and be joined with them. Being in a tribe of wealthy people will eventually make you start thinking like a wealthy person. Meanwhile, being in a tribe of poor people will also make you start thinking poorly. If you don't desire to be successful, then all you have to do is to be around those who are not successful.

But I believe you want to be successful. I believe you are not ready to settle for less, then you should work something out for yourself. Upgrade your mind, upgrade your relationship, and upgrade your result.

I believe in you.

DAY 14
WHAT IS YOUR ONE THING?

In my twenties, I used to pride myself on being a multi-talented multitasker. I could do so many things, and I tend to do most of them at the same time.

I once had on my CV - *'I'm a multi-tasker par excellence. I can multitask at the highest level of precision and accuracy.'* Don't ask me where I got that line from.

The interesting thing was, I was getting lots of praise from people who were using me.

But I was not effective in any of those things I was doing. I was not making an impact or influence and significance seemed very far away.

Why am I sharing this with you?

Beloved, please reject the lure of being a multitasker, especially at the start of your purpose journey.

The praise of men can be very tempting but most of the people praising you are just using you.

To make an impact and be influential, you first have to be known for one thing.

Go and ask anyone you know who is great today, they started with their one thing.

I love the words of Paul the Apostle, ' *...but this one thing I do...*' Philippians 3:13 KJV.

So, what is your one thing?

One of the surest ways to live a purposeful life is to start with one thing.

Find your most dominant gift, focus on it, commit to it, and build a personal brand on it.

When that one thing becomes successful, people will naturally trust any other of your expressions.

But when starting, focus is key to building something of significance, worthwhile, and lasting.

Again, what is your one thing?

I believe in you.

DAY 15

YOU CAN NOT FULFILL PURPOSE ALONE

It is impossible to fulfill your purpose in isolation because no one grows in isolation.

When God was done creating Adam, He said, ' ...*It is not good that the man should be alone; I will make him an help meet for him.' Genesis 2:18 KJV.*

This means it is not the plan of God for you to fulfill His purpose for your life in isolation. In the journey of life, God will deliberately bring people around your life, those are people who will contribute to the success of your achievement and purpose fulfillment. Don't make the mistake of thinking you can do it alone, you can't do it all alone. If Adam could do it alone, then God would not have given him Eve. If Abraham could do it alone, God would not have given him Sarah.

Go and check some of those people who are doing well in any field of life, they are people who joined themselves with others. You can be born alone by your parents, but you cannot grow up alone. Growth happens with the contributions of other people. There is no special way to better grow than allowing other people to contribute meaningfully to your life. If you understand the principles of growing with other people, then you will move faster and better in your life's journey. No wonder the scripture says,

'Two are better than one, Because they have a good reward for their labor.' Ecclesiastes 4:9 NKJV.

Two are better than one. That's a powerful scripture, but you should also note that even though the Bible says two are better than one, it does not mean you should associate yourself with anybody who is not ready to contribute something to your life. Two good heads are better. It is rather better to be alone and keep searching for the good one than to be with the wrong person.

You can't fulfill your purpose all alone, no one grows in isolation. You will need the contributions of others to achieve your goals and plans in life. No matter how skilled and talented you may be, you will always need the contribution of other people around you. You may be effective though, but to be more effective, you will need others. You can't succeed in isolation. Successful people don't succeed alone. Some people were not doing well in their business endeavours until they got one or more partners who also contributed their quota to the success of the business. So, you are going to need people to fulfill your purpose effectively.

And if you need people, then you must know how to work with people to be effective. Working with other people is a skill and it can be developed, but I noticed that a lot of people don't even know how to keep relationships. To make other people work with you, you must cultivate your relationship skills so that they can get along with you.

I want to share with you seven things you must do with people to fulfill your purpose effectively:

1. Love people
The Bible says, *'Owe no man anything, but to love one another...'*(Romans 13:8 KJV). You cannot fulfill your purpose if you don't love people. You must genuinely love people. When you love people, you will make room for them in your life, accommodate them, and acknowledge their uniqueness. Meanwhile, in loving those around you, you should make sure that your love has no bias. If your love has a bias, you may slow down the effectiveness of other people around you.

2. Value people
Every man has something valuable to offer but beyond what they can offer you, learn to value people. To value people is to take an interest in them and their growth. Respect people,

never take anyone for granted, and appreciate them. Even if they are your subordinates, you must still value them, and let them know you value them. Acknowledge them publicly if you can - let them know you don't take their roles in your life for granted.

3. Believe in people

You will not be where you are today if no one believes in you. So, make it your duty to believe in people. Believe the best of and about them. Even at their worst state, learn to be hopeful about their future. Always acknowledge the fact that no one is perfect, so even if people around you make or commit some errors, make sure you are willing to forgive them and still believe in them. Believing in people will make you gain their loyalty and this, in turn, will make them to effectively work for you more.

4. Invest in people

This one is so crucial to the fulfillment of your purpose in life. Zig Ziglar would often say, 'You can have everything in life you want if you will just help other people get what they want.' He's right! If you add value to people, your value will keep going up. Make people better when they meet you. Don't leave people worse than they were. Commit to adding value to people daily.

5. Honour people

We live in a generation that is gradually losing the culture of honour. Honour people by regarding them as not any less than you. Even if they are younger than you or have not achieved as much as you have achieved in life, still honour them. Honour their time, their space, and their decisions. And if they are older than you, please honour them. There is such a transfer of blessing that comes with honouring our elders. Don't go with the waves of dishonour. That's common in our generation. It won't get you anywhere. You may not agree with everyone but honour everyone.

6. Care for people
Being there for people is also one of those things you'd hardly see in our world. We're gradually losing the culture of being available for each other. Truth is, in the words of John C Maxwell, 'No one cares how much you know until they know how much you care.' Care for people. Life does not just revolve around you. I know life can be quite busy but once in a while, check on your friends, reach out to them, make time for them, speak their love language, and do your best to connect with them. Forgive them when they offend you.

7. Listen to people
We live in a world where there is so much noise around and it's hard to hear ourselves, but we must be intentional about listening to people. We must listen to their hurts, pains, desires, and constructive feedback. Don't be full of yourself such that you don't take feedback. Learn to listen! There is a reason God gave us two ears and one mouth.

The list is not exhaustive, so I am sure you can add more to it. So, go ahead. What would you add?

I believe in you.

DAY 16
THE POWER OF COMMITMENT

When we think about Ruth in the Bible, we often think about how God turned her life around when she remarried but we don't often talk about her as a very committed woman.

The first time Ruth demonstrated her commitment was when Naomi, her mother-in-law, asked her to go back.

Her sister-in-law had kissed Naomi and left. Naomi pleaded with Ruth to do the same. In her words, '**Look...** *"your sister-in-law is going back to her people and her gods. Go back with her."*' (Ruth 1:15 NIV).

Ruth's response is worth studying for days:

> *'... "Don't urge me to leave you or to turn back from you. Where you go I will go, and where you stay I will stay. Your people will be my people and your God my God. Where you die I will die, and there I will be buried. May the Lord deal with me, be it ever so severely, if even death separates you and me."'*
>
> *Ruth 1:16-17 NIV.*

There is no other test of commitment than someone putting their own lives on the line.

I read this scripture recently, and when I got to the part where Ruth said, 'Where you die, I will die,' I lost it!

I was like, was that statement even worth it? But it shows a woman who was ruthlessly committed to a cause she believed in.

Naomi realised this because it was recorded that when Naomi realised that Ruth was determined to go with her, she stopped urging her.

The truth is that genuine commitment cannot go unnoticed. You must be committed to something. One of the reasons a lot of people are not successful can be traced to the fact that they are not committed to something; they have too many things they are doing; they are never committed to one thing. Some people have several mentors, but they are never committed to one person. Let's take for instance, if an individual is committed to more than one person in a marital relationship, will that person ever have a blissful home? No, it is not possible.

Ruth was so committed to the family of her husband that she would not allow her mother to go even after the death of her husband. The second time we saw Ruth's wholeheartedness was when she took the initiative to get work to source food for her and her mother-in-law.

In her words, '... ***"Let me go to the fields and pick up the leftover grain behind anyone in whose eyes I find favour."***'
Ruth 2:2 NIV.

No one asked her to do it but due to her commitment to Naomi, she took the initiative. Not only that, when she got to the field, the workers of Boaz noticed her commitment too. They told Boaz about her, '***...She came into the field and has remained here from morning till now, except for a short rest in the shelter.***' *(Ruth 2:7 NIV).*

Are you this devoted to the purpose of God for your life? Are you ruthlessly committed to your life's assignment? Or are you one leg in, one leg out? Are you there today, and nowhere to be found tomorrow?

Let me ask you another question: do you want to fulfill God's mandate for your life and be a success in it? Then you must be committed to finding that purpose and also commit yourself to fulfill that purpose. Showing commitment to your purpose shows how serious and deliberate you are in making your life work. I have seen people who started a particular business and because it's not giving them the right result in a very short time, they quit, stop the business, and start another business.

After a while, they quit that very business too because they felt it was not paying them much, started another business and that's how they've been doing all their lives. Such people can never climb the ladder of greatness because they are not committed to one course.

When you want to stay and remain committed to a particular course, you must not engage yourself with guesswork, be certain about what you want to start and commit yourself to it full-time because fulfilling God's purpose for your life is not something you will do on a part-time basis. You must engage in it full-time and commit yourself to it.

God wants you to show commitment to His purpose for your life. Let the story of Ruth encourage you. Her commitment earned her inclusion in the lineage of Jesus.

To be committed also means to be diligent. You must diligently soak yourself with the assignment God has given to you to fulfill. Don't confuse yourself with what other people are doing out there. What others are doing might look good and great, but when you also stay committed and stay in your lane, what you're doing will also be excellent.

There is a great reward in commitment, it may not pay off at the start, but the reward in there is worth it at the end. Jesus came out of the lineage of Ruth because of her commitment. Just assume she went her way just like the other wife to marry another man, the Savior wouldn't have come from her lineage. Ruth at that time might not understand the gravity of what she was doing. It may not even make sense to her, but in the end, what she did had a positive effect on her life.

You may not understand the essence of staying committed to your purpose today, but it will surely pay off tomorrow. People may not even take note of the great work you are doing at the moment, but it will pay off for you in years to come. I want to encourage you to stay committed and keep grinding until you get there.

God is surely a rewarder of our commitment and devotion to Him.

I believe in you.

DAY 17
YOU MAY NOT FEEL QUALIFIED

Some years ago, I was asked to teach a course that I didn't have much experience or knowledge in.

The Professor who gave me the task simply said to me, 'Samuel, I believe you can teach the course, so go and learn all that you need to learn. You are teaching it.'

I read the course outline and some of the previous content of the course, and I shivered. I was afraid! It didn't help that I got to the classroom, and I, the lecturer, was the youngest and least experienced.

It was an evening class, so it had all these grey-haired men and women, who came from their respective offices seeking to learn more to upgrade their knowledge and consequently their careers.

You must understand that I have no previous experience in the Information Technology field.

I asked my students to introduce themselves, and the least experienced had been in the Information Technology field for at least five years.

My fear came back.

When I ended up introducing myself, I could only mention my Ph.D. degree which I had only just earned.

I had to put a disclaimer saying, 'I understand that all of you are older and perhaps more experienced than I am but my job is to facilitate this class in such a way that we all end up learning from each other.'

I must say it turned out to be one of the best classes I ever taught.

Why am I sharing this with you?

Sometimes, you may not feel qualified for what God has called you to do, but that should not deter you. The most important thing is that He who sent you believes in you.

Once you have God's approval, He is your sufficiency, and that alone is enough recipe for confidence. The truth is that most times, God won't call and choose the qualified, He will call those He wants to use and qualify them for the job. You are not in the position to tell God what He should do with your life, you should rather be ready to please Him and do whatever He wants you to do. Don't feel unqualified, just allow your confidence to be in Him and you will be able to do everything He has called you to do. I love the words of the Apostle Paul:

'I can do all things through Christ who strengthens me.' Philippians 4:13 NKJV.

You are not the one who sent yourself, so you cannot empower yourself, nor can you strengthen yourself, but the One who called and chose you is able and capable of giving you the required strengths and experiences you need for all He has called you to do. Stop feeling unqualified for what God has already qualified you to do. You should step into your mandate, into your purpose, and your calling. The day you should step into it is today, not tomorrow.

I also love the words of Paul to the Corinthians when he said, *'Not that we are sufficient of ourselves to think of anything as being from ourselves, but our sufficiency is from God, who also made us sufficient as ministers of the new covenant, not of the letter but of the Spirit; for the letter kills, but the Spirit gives life.' 2 Corinthians 3:5-6 NKJV.*

I also love another part of his letter where he said, *'Brothers and sisters, think of what you were when you were called. Not many of you were wise by human standards; not many were influential; not many were of noble birth. But God chose the foolish things of the world to shame the wise; God chose the weak things of the world to shame the strong. God chose the lowly things of this world and the despised things—and the things that are not—to nullify the things that are, so that no one may boast before him. 1 Corinthians 1:26-29 NIV.*

You may not look like the one God is calling and sending.

You may not speak with great eloquence like Moses.

You may even be shy.

You may be inexperienced.

You may not have a lot of money.

Not many people believe you can do it, including you.

Listen, what God has called you to do, He will give you the grace and power to do it. Moses couldn't lead the Israelites out of Egypt, he saw himself as an unqualified man. He didn't see anything good about himself. It came to a time when he was giving excuses to God. God did not because of his shortcomings replace him, He rather gave him Aaron as support.

God will give you support for the work He has called you to do, so you don't need to worry about how you will fulfill that purpose, carry out the assignment, or fulfill the mandate, just make sure you are ready to do the work. It is God that will help you, not humans, so put all worries and anxieties on Him.

' Cast your cares on the LORD and he will sustain you; he will never let the righteous be shaken.' Psalm 55:22 NIV.

When you feel inadequate or unqualified, it is an opportunity for God to show himself strong on your behalf. The fact that you felt unqualified will give God the reason to make you qualified so that you can remain humble to carry out the assignment He had given to you to carry out. Normally, you should not feel qualified to do God's work. Feeling qualified can bring pride and arrogance into your life. You should rather see yourself as a vessel who is not qualified but ready to do the job.

Let me close this chapter with the below scripture:

'Now to him who is able to do immeasurably more than all we ask or imagine, according to his power that is at work within us.' Ephesians 3:20 NIV.

I believe in you.

DAY 18

BIG DREAMS EQUAL BIG PRICE

I took my car for repairs recently, then I was told it was time to replace the four tires. When the mechanic told me how much it would cost to replace the tires, I was stunned.

I bought this car about a year before this incident. It's considerably bigger than my previous car. When I had to change the tires for my previous car, what I paid was very cheap. This time, I've been asked to bring almost four times that amount.

That was when I made a realisation that there is a correlation between size and price. I mean, if you have a big dream, you will have to pay a big price for it.

A small dream won't cost you much but a big dream will cost you so much.

The interesting thing about the price you have to pay, though, is that you can never bargain on the price to pay for your dream. And you have to pay the price in advance. Even before you see any result, you have to start paying the price. No price is too high to pay for your dream, no sacrifice is too much to make your dreams come to fruition. If you have big dreams, you must be ready to do big work. Any big dream without big work is a mere wish and fantasy.

Don't be a daydreamer, don't just dream for dreaming sake. You must be ready to pay the dues, if not, your dream will not pass the roof of your house.

The Wright brothers dreamt that something could fly in the air that could also convey people from one destination to another. No one believed in them, but they believed it could happen. With serious hard work, tenacity, and great commitment to the dream they had, they were able to achieve it. They paid the price for their innovation to see the light of the day.

Most of the innovations you see out there today are innovations of people who paid the price years ago; people who refused to give up on what they dreamt about, but were willing to give all that it would take to bring the dreams to manifestation.

You don't need any prophet to tell you whether your dreams will come to a reality or not, the way you are handling the dream today will tell whether that dream will come to a reality tomorrow.

YOUR PURPOSE WILL COST YOU EVERYTHING!

You need to understand that big dreams will also require big responsibility. To take responsibility is to take charge, which means no one will come to help you fulfill your dream, you must be ready to put in the hard work. You must also be resilient because obstacles would come up that may hinder your fulfillment of those dreams, but you must also stand against them just to make sure that your dreams become a reality.

One of the major keys to success in life and the fulfillment of purpose is to find the price to pay for it and determine to pay it.

You must be ready to pay it in advance through sacrifices, learning and growing, consistency, perseverance, resilience, pain, and so on.

That big dream will not happen for cheap. There is a price to pay.

I believe in you.

DAY 19

NO ONE IS BETTER THAN YOU

I have a friend who is quite well off financially. I remember in our early days of friendship, I used to think he was proud. The truth is, if you didn't understand him, you would think he is quite arrogant or proud when he talks about his life and what God has helped him to achieve.

While I was not as well to do as he was financially, and later coming to understand him more, I made sure to never misconstrue the things he shared with me. I welcomed them, listened carefully, and enjoyed every bit of our conversations.

I was in an intentional process of working on my money/financial mindset at the time. So, I was like a sponge, soaking in all he had to say because I knew I had so much to learn from him if I was going to get to where I wanted to be financially.

I never argued, I just listened and learned. Sometimes, on the other end of the phone, I was taking notes.

Days, months, and years have gone by and my money mindset has changed a lot because of our friendship, and other people like him in my life. His mindset has rubbed off on me. Now, we think alike financially, whereas, at the beginning, it was not so.

Why am I sharing this with you? For three reasons:

1. **The people you move with determine what you attract or repel in your life.**

If you move with the right people, you will attract the right things and develop the right mindset. If you move with the wrong people, you will also attract the wrong things and the wrong mindset, and it's only a matter of time before you are doomed.

No wonder the book of Proverbs in the Bible says, "He who walks with wise men will be wise, but the companion of fools will suffer harm" (Proverbs 13:20). That scripture is very powerful. I mean, it would have been logical to say the companion of fools will become more foolish but it goes on to say, "the companion of fools will suffer harm". The wrong relationship will cost you in a detremental way but the right relationship is a multiplier in your life.

2. No one is better than you, they are only doing better.

So, when you meet people who are doing better than you, grab your pen and journal, it's a season of learning. You will do yourself a disservice trying to compete with them or becoming jealous of them. It does not matter if they are younger than you, or your age mate, you can learn from anyone doing better than you. It's harder to learn from someone you are competing with, than from someone you have submitted to their mentorship humbly. The latter is always the wise way to go.

Whatever price you need to pay to learn from people who are doing better than you and be in their presence/circle, please pay it. Should the price be monetary, do not hesitate to pay it. If you can't afford the price monetarily, ask what you else (that won't comprise your godly values) you can do to learn from them. One hour with such people can save you one year of stress and hustling.

3. Be intentional about working on your mindset every single day.

This will help you become intentional about the people you meet. Due to this consciousness, you could almost immediately tell who should mentor you, who should be your friend, and who you should mentor too.

This will also help you in developing yourself into a person of value capable of attracting other valuable people too.

I believe in you.

DAY 20

AVAILABILITY

In the last few weeks, to the glory of God, I've met at least five people who said God told them to work with me in one capacity or the other.

Some signed up for my coaching, others for my writing Bootcamp, and some other of my programmes.

I was reflecting recently on why God would send these people to me, and one word came to me; availability!

There are more gifted people than me - better coaches, speakers, and thought leaders but they have failed to make themselves available.

I have come to discover a trait about God, He is not out for the best or perfect person. He is often seeking the available.

That's why one question God is always asking is, 'Whom shall I send?' Moses himself felt unqualified and imperfect when God first called him. He gave several excuses as to why he was not good enough to be a leader. God is sovereign in His dealing with people and He will always use people based on their availability, not their capability. The best thing you can do for yourself right now is to make yourself available for God to use. Even if you think you aren't good enough to do the work, just make yourself available; it is availability that will birth capability.

God is throwing the opportunity open to anyone who chooses to be available and responsible. You are part of the men God wants to use to fulfill His purpose in this end time and He is calling you into the fold so you can start making things happen in His kingdom. The door is always open and God is always calling people. One amazing fact about God is that He will never chase you away. Once you make yourself available for Him, then He furnishes you with everything you need for the assignment. One havoc you can cause to yourself is to hold yourself back or run away from His mandate for your life. You don't have to run away, just come and make yourself available. A man called Jonah in the Bible tried all he could to run away from his purpose, God sent a big fish to swallow him for three days. You can imagine that!

'Now the LORD had prepared a great fish to swallow Jonah. And Jonah was in the belly of the fish three days and three nights.' Jonah 1:17 NKJV.

You don't need to run away, just determine to do the work, make yourself available and you will see how God will empower you to do the work.

If I am not available to help people in the various capacities God has helped me to, He wouldn't send them to me. When you also make yourself available for God to use, He will send you people who are paramount for the assignment He has given you to do.

I always say that ability without availability is a disability. God cannot do anything with you unless you choose to be available.

To be available is to realise you are not perfect but you will show up anyway.

To be available is to not look at your flaws and still shine your light anyway.

To be available is to not feel like doing it but still push yourself to do it.

To be available is to leverage every idea or assignment God has given you and birth them.

To be available is to serve sacrificially with love.

Always remember, God does the impossible only with the available.

I believe in you.

DAY 21
THE POWER OF WORDS

'Samuel, I have a problem. When I was about five years old, my father and I would wrestle (that was how his father played with him and his brother).

And obviously, he would easily wrestle me to the floor and say these words, "You are a bum. You will always be a bum."' (Meaning: you're a loser and you will always be a loser).

He is probably in his mid to late 50s but those words have haunted him since and they still do.

He said no matter how much he tries to achieve anything; those words would come back to him and he'd feel he doesn't deserve any of his successes.

He has low self-esteem as a result and really doesn't believe he can achieve much in life.

We spoke endlessly and I believe I was able to help him. I shared with him how he could change that story of his.

But that's not what I want to share with you today, I wanted to share a few lessons from his story:

1. Be careful of the words you allow people to sow into your life. Words are seeds and your mind/soul is (a very fertile) soil. Reject what is not good for you and accept what is good for your mind. Every word spoken into someone's life has the tendency to grow into a big world. Spoken words are so powerful that they are able to destroy and mend lives. Those who live carelessly with words are only playing with fire, and the funniest part is that you cannot be unintentional with words; whatever you say from your mouth takes deep root the moment you speak them from your mouth.

The words you speak are flesh, whether you mean what you say or not.

'And the Word became flesh and dwelt among us...' John 1:14a NKJV.

Whatever words you speak into your life will eventually live with you in the end. It may take a long time before you begin to notice the manifestation though, but they are coming back to live with you. This is why it is rather essential to be mindful of your words; your words form your worth.

2. Parents, be careful what you say to your children. Don't hurt their future through your careless words. I have seen parents using abusive words and insults to relate with their children. You may not see or notice the effects of what you are doing at the moment but can I tell you something? You are only hurting the future of those children. If you truly want your children to excel, you must be deliberate about speaking good words into their lives.

So many children are battling with an inferiority complex today because of what their parents said to them years ago. You cannot escape the consequences of your words. Speak well and all will be well with your children, speak doom and everything will go wrong with your children. Do you know you can shape the destinies of your children by what you constantly say to them? Yes, you can! This is why you should not just utter statements that will bring them down. Instead of speaking negatively to them, speak positively into their lives. Instead of abusing or cursing them, bless them and wait for what you've been saying because your words will soon be moulding them into the kind of children you want them to be.

3. Nothing ruins potential more than low self-esteem and the opinions of others. If you have these two traits in your life, please get all the help you need. Low self-esteem has harmed a lot of people and still harms lots of people today. Some people are not scared of doing big things, but low self-esteem is bringing them down. Others will not do anything worthwhile if they have not sought the opinions of others. Such people

will quickly withdraw into their shells, especially when they notice people are not endorsing what they are doing. If you are the type that is battling with low self-esteem syndrome, you need to get rid of it before it gets rid of you. You should take charge of your life and begin to do something worthwhile, if not, you will not be able to fulfill God's mandate for your life.

God has deposited so much in you, hence you must do everything and anything to use everything He has deposited in you. Don't allow low self-esteem and people's opinions to take you down. I charge you to be in charge of your life and start doing what God has sent you to do. If you are the type that is battling with low self-esteem, send me a message for a start.

4. No one has the right to call you what God hasn't named you. Let me say that again another way, people's opinion of you should not be your reality. You should be confident about what God has called you to be. You must not allow people's opinions about your person to bring you down. After God, you are the next god of your life and at that, you're the next creator of your life. No one anywhere, regardless of who they are, has the right to call you what you are not. If people start calling you what you are not, you can refute it, reject it, and despise it. You are not to take upon yourself the name God has not called you.

Let me tell you something, God has called you a success, and no one has the right to tag you as a failure, even if it is obvious that you are failing at something. No one has the right to tag you as poor because God has made you prosper. No one will come to fight for you, you must fight for yourself and take what belongs to you. You are blessed, so if anyone tags you cursed, don't accept it, reject it and pray against it. Your reality is in what God has said about you, not what people are saying about you.

5. Any words, or opinions that you have allowed into you before now can be renounced. Every day, repeat and affirm to yourself the exact opposite of those opinions or declarations. Very soon, your reality would change. Though words are powerful and any word spoken will immediately take root if care is not taken, opposing and negative words can be reversed. If anyone speaks negative utterances or words into your life, you can reverse them by the Word of God. There are a bunch of promises for you in the Scripture; you can always use the Word of God to re-affirm and confirm what God has spoken to you.

Tell yourself things like, 'I am great,' 'I am blessed,' 'I am prosperous,' 'I am healthy,' 'I am better,' and so on. Don't accept negative words, refute them, any destroyed foundation can be rebuilt. Yes, rebuild your life with your words, your words are powerful.

6. If your life has been stagnant, retrogressive, or dreadful, think deeply about some of the opinions that have been sown into you. Take stock of them and do the needful (number 1 above). Your life should not be stagnated, you should

empower yourself to move forward. No one can re-write the stories of your life except you. If you want to move on and move forward, you should take charge of your life right now and do the needful.

7. Only God determines your potential and what you can achieve. And guess what? Your potential in God is infinite. You can achieve anything you set your mind to achieve. Always remember that you are unstoppable, you are well able to do and achieve a lot if you set your mind to them. Your levels and height in life can only be determined by God, no man can set any limitations for you unless you set one for yourself. Hence, you are infinite, unlimited, and unstoppable!

You can do all things through Christ. Don't believe the lies anymore. You are more than the opinions of people about you. Begin, this day, to live above your unpleasant circumstances.

Stay blessed.

I believe in you.

DAY 22
BE MINDFUL

Recently, my computer started misbehaving, becoming so slow and frustrating to work with. I do a lot of things on my computer, so the frustration became a daily affair.

I told my wife I would have to change it soon but she kept on encouraging me to troubleshoot it.

So, I heeded her advice and decided to look into the memory and check what was going on. To my amazement, some of the powerful programmes on my computer including the ones I use in editing photos and videos had stored up Gigabytes of unwanted files and I didn't even know.

The moment I deleted all of those files, my computer was back to normal again. I fell in love with it again. Hahaha!

My point is that now and then, we need to troubleshoot our lives to make sure there are no unwanted deposits, or things that slow us down or frustrate us, leaving us wishing we had another life instead.

Check for those programmes that have left some unwanted baggage, and deposits that are now making your life, career, marriage, relationships, ministry, purpose, business, etc. unbearable.

Take some time off. Go on a retreat somewhere, and have some alone time to think and reflect. Most times, some of the challenges we encounter in life will only require us to create a special time for ourselves to reflect and meditate upon the events of our lives to be able to find a solution. You need to start minding how the events of your life unfold. Also, be mindful of some of those activities that are not helpful to your life and scrap them away. Your life should not be filled with junk and unwanted things.

For instance, you planted a crop and as the crop is growing, unwanted grass starts growing up with it. If you don't take care of those unwanted grasses or get rid of them, they will choke and destroy your good crop. There are some unwanted thoughts, imagination, and even activities that you are engaging with right now that are not supposed to be in your life; you need to get rid of them so that your life can experience some freedom.

Take some time out for yourself, go on a vacation, go on a personal retreat, be alone, take up the Word of God, and treat your mind. Let me tell you something, if you can treat your mind well, your life will take a new shape. You can always be anywhere in the world. You can do anything you set your heart to do, just take care of your mind.

Junks, negative thoughts, and imaginations are not good for you. They are not healthy for you, get a way of uprooting them. Be intentional about everything that you allow into your mind. Take note of what you feed your heart with because junk may feel sweet and good to the mouth, but they are not good for the body. So, that negative thought and imagination may seem good to you today, but they are causing havoc in your life slowly. Start getting rid of them from today. Though you may not be able to get rid of them in a day, start doing it today and make sure you get rid of them completely before they completely ruin you. If you find any junk in your mind, take intentional, mindful, and conscious steps to remove them.

If they are bad habits, you would need to install new habits as replacements.

If they are people, you may need to sever those relationships. Whatever they are, take conscious steps to remove them from your life.

I believe in you.

DAY 23
STOP DABBLING INTO THINGS

Why do you think we ask people to be mature (at least well-advanced in age and thinking) before they get married?

What do you think? It's simple; to have a successful marriage or relationship, the first thing to look for is not a partner.

In the same way, if you want to be rich, the first thing to look for is not money. To have a successful business, the first thing to do is not to start a business.

Also, to have a successful life, it's not just about dabbling into things. The first thing to do to be successful at anything is to build the mentality of success in that area.

So, how do you build the mentality of success? You got the answer - Learning.

No bird will ever build a nest in a vacuum, every bird will build their nest on the tree branch. Before they start building the nest, they will make sure the tree is strong enough to hold the nest and other birds that will stay in it.

A lot of people are building their lives, businesses, and even marriages on emptiness. This is why a lot of people crash a few months or years into something. Just as the bird will not build its nest on a weak branch of a tree, so you can't afford to build your business or live on a weak foundation. To have a solid building or mansion, the foundation must be thick and solid, if not, the building would collapse in the long run.

If you build anything on a weak foundation, that thing will collapse. This is one of the challenges of those starting businesses today. Those who refuse to learn and understand how business works will not succeed in business because they have refused to learn how it works. The same applies to marriage, you can't just make up your mind to get married because you think all your mates and colleagues are already getting married and you must get married too. That's a wrong foundation to start with. You must learn from people who have been in the business of marriage for a while. You can get books, go to seminars, get their podcasts, and so on to learn about how marriage works.

You can't just dabble into things and expect a better result, it's not done that way. The fact remains that there is a template of success in the areas of things you want to do. If you want to start a business, there is a person already doing that same business, go to such a person and learn from them. I don't think there is a new business out there. Even though people are coming up with new ideas daily, however, there are people out there who already are doing the very business you are trying to start. So it is with marriage, your success in marriage depends solely upon the degree of your learning. If you refuse to learn how your business works, then you will have to learn the hard way. But you can cut yourself the stress of learning the hard way by approaching those who have already tried what you are trying to do.

'For which of you, intending to build a tower, does not sit down first and count the cost, whether he has enough to finish it.' Luke 14:28 NKJV.

That's the scripture for you. To count the cost means to first sit down and plan, learn, know what it will take you to start a business, know and understand what it means to get married, etc. A lot of people still don't understand that marriage is hard work, but they just dabble into it, expecting everything to go on smoothly and rosy, only to now discover that they won't be able to cope with the stress and work of marriage.

Now, what should you do?

1. ***Learn from the experience of others.***

How do you learn from others? Through books, podcasts, video and audio programmes, mentorship, coaching, workshops, schools, etc. There are lots of courses and content on YouTube from experts in any field. You can go to learn from people who are already doing what you are doing. There is no subject you are seeking on YouTube that you won't find. Instead of playing with ignorance and failure, it is rather better to learn and be a better person.

Meanwhile, you can also pay for courses. There are several coaches in your field of endeavour out there, you can always learn from them. Don't try to do things on your own without having prior knowledge of that thing. Don't just take unnecessary risks! It can be very costly sometimes to learn from your experience. The worst way to learn is to ignore the experiences of others and choose to experience the same failures others have. It's a dangerous move. I have seen this in many youths today. They want to fail on their own. They even argue with their parents - ' Allow me to make my own mistakes.'

My point is that any mistake you can avoid by learning from others is wisdom.

2. *Learn by taking action.*
From time to time, you read things, you hear things from your mentors and leaders about how they succeed. You will be doing yourself a disservice by not taking action on those things.

You owe it to yourself and your destiny to give those things a try and if they work, you keep doing them, if they don't, you don't keep doing them. People have underrated the act of taking action as part of the criterion for succeeding in life. Nothing moves if you don't first move!

It is not enough to learn, you must by all means put into practice or action those things you have learnt. Don't just learn, don't just acquire knowledge, take action. If you don't take action, you will not get results. It is an action that births result. The person praying to get married in a month's time, who is not in any relationship, who is not also ready to be a friend of the opposite gender is only daydreaming. Take inspired action, even if you will make mistakes. Just know that you will pick up from where you failed. I'm not talking about expensive mistakes.

But not trying at all is limiting.

DAY 24
ENVISION YOUR LIFE AS A SPORT

Imagine watching a soccer game where both teams refuse to take a shot at goal. I doubt you will sit for the entire 90 minutes. It'd be such a boring game to watch. The essence of any game is the goals.

No matter what sport it is, all eyes are on the goal and the scoreboard. If no team is taking a shot at goal, it's not worth watching.

Envision your life as a sport, or a game. Are you taking shots at life or are you always on the defensive? Too many people are on the defensive side of life.

They get an idea and instead of them to take a shot at it, they begin asking:

What if people don't like the idea?

What if my friends hate me for it?

What if it doesn't sell?

What if this, what if that?

This is the major source of mediocrity in life. The truth is, no one is coming from anywhere to help you do what you can do for yourself. If you are not aiming at a goal in life, life will be like a mystery to you and when you feel or think life is a mystery, then you will soon begin to see yourself as a miserable person. A lot of people are in that ocean today, and they can't come out again. They are there because they feel people won't accept them, they feel they are not loved. They consider people's opinions and that marks the end of their race in life.

The question is, do you have a place you are going? If yes, then set goals on how to get there and start going. You may not get to that goal earlier, but make sure you are always on the run. Don't make the mistake of thinking people will accept you, endorse, and appraise you when you are on the move. No, they won't! They will rather see why you should not do it. Don't plan to end up as a miserable being. Envision your life as a sport, set goals for yourself, and keep your eye on that hefty goal.

'I press toward the goal for the prize of the upward call of God in Christ Jesus.' Philippians 3:14 NKJV.

Learn from Apostle Paul who was seeing a prize before himself, so he set himself to get at the goal. You must also press through because if you don't press through, you will not break through! Don't be afraid of setting those goals and moving towards them. It is only when you start that roads will start clearing for you.

So, you have failed to apply for that job because you think you are not good enough; go and submit your application letter tomorrow, apply for it. If you are not the best for the job, then who else is? You deserve it and that is why you must be bold enough to approach that company to submit your application letter. You have refused to take that opportunity because you believe it's not meant for people like you.

Henceforth, stop making the mistake of thinking better things are reserved for a special and specific set of people, no! You also deserve better things. You deserve to earn six and seven figures. You deserve to sleep in a seven-star hotel. You deserve a better house, a better car, and so on. Grab those opportunities that are coming your way because you deserve them. You must not neglect or reject great opportunities again. You deserve them, that is why they are coming across your path.

I pray for you, that those opportunities you've missed and lost are coming to you soon, in Jesus' name.

Listen, if you are not taking shots at life, you will soon be relegated to life's bench. If proper care is not taken, you will soon be relegated out of life and nobody will even know someone like you exists.

I challenge you to take a shot at life this year, reawaken yourself, take those opportunities, and move on with the good things of life.

Have you been on the defensive all year long or are you on the offensive?

How many ideas have you started?

How many courses have you gone for?

How many books have you read?

Have you tried to discover your purpose?

How many investments have you made?

Did you apply for that promotion?

Did you set goals?

Have you made a vision board yet?

Or are you full of excuses?

Time waits for no one and life will pass you by if all you do is stay on the defensive all the time. People who stay on the defensive all their lives always end up regretting.

I pray that won't be you.

I believe in you.

DAY 25
DON'T REJECT KNOWLEDGE

It is dangerous to not know, and not know that/what you don't know.

It reminds me of an Arabian proverb I saw online some years back:

He who knows not,
and knows not that he knows not,
is a fool; shun him.
He who knows not,
and knows that he knows not,
is a student; teach him.
He who knows,
and knows not that he knows,

is asleep; wake him.
He who knows,
and knows that he knows,
is wise; follow him.

Let's shed more light on the person who doesn't know what he doesn't know. The proverb calls this person a fool. Do you know why? That's the highest form of ignorance. This level of ignorance leads to destruction.

This is the level of Ignorance in the Book of *Hosea 4:6 KJV*: **'My people are destroyed for lack of knowledge: because thou hast rejected knowledge, I will also reject thee…'**

The key is found in the latter part of that verse, *'because you have rejected knowledge'*

Rejecting knowledge means you know what to do to change your life but you refuse to do it.

You know you need to set goals, but at this current time, you have set no goal.

You know you are to read books, yet at this time, you have hardly read one book.

You know you are to attend seminars, workshops, and coaching sessions to help you become better but you choose not to.

You have a million excuses, 10,000 reasons why you cannot afford the knowledge you need and you're surprised your life is going backwards.

No one rejects knowledge and gets better, you are responsible for making sure that you go for knowledge and get better with yourself. There is a popular saying in my place that says, 'What the bird eats is what will also enable the bird to fly in the sky.' And that's the truth, if the bird is hungry for food, the bird won't have the strength to fly.

So, it is with you that if you refuse to gather adequate knowledge that will enable you to fly higher tomorrow, then you may remain at a spot without adding any meaning to your life. You need to stop living a mediocre life and start living an impactful life. Go for knowledge. If it will take you to spend and invest all your earnings to get knowledge, please do it.

'Wisdom is the principal thing; Therefore get wisdom. And in all your getting, get understanding.' Proverbs 4:7 NKJV.

What the above scripture is saying is to get wisdom at all costs. Even if it will cost you a fortune, just make sure you get it. Because it will save you in the future. If you are the type that hates reading, then you are in for a shock; your peers will leave you behind, and you will eventually become outdated. If you are the type that cannot afford to sign up for a course or seminar because it will involve a registration fee, then I'm sorry for you because doom might come looking for you in the future.

As far as you are concerned, I want to urge you to improve yourself, do all you can to spend money on your mind. Upgrade yourself, go back to school, go and sharpen your skill as an entrepreneur, and go for your Master's degree or Ph.D. degree if that's what will make you stay on top of your game. Just upgrade yourself and stay up there. People who don't constantly learn will not climb to the top of their life's ladder. Be committed to making your life better.

The truth is, no one will come from outside to motivate or tell you to improve yourself or upgrade your skills. But you are getting the motivation to do it from this chapter, don't ignore this call, go for it, and be your self-motivator. If no one will tell you to improve yourself, please tell yourself and take the right steps because you are better off when you know better.

Stop rejecting knowledge and watch your life take a whole new turn. No one who is in a continuous mode of learning will ever go down. If you are constantly learning new things every day, your life will be better for it. There are several great materials out there that will improve your mental life, and mindset and they will help you reshape the way you think.

Most of the time, the only factor that is bringing a lot of people down is their mindset, and the way they think. You will never rise above the level of your thinking. It is still a lack of knowledge that is making some people think in a certain way. If you find anyone operating with a mediocre mindset, that person will never do anything better than what he has always been doing. But the moment that person is curious to know how to act, live, and do things better, then the person's life will start taking a new shape.

You should go for more knowledge, don't roast yourself in the boiling oil of foolishness, learn more, get more materials, get a coach or a mentor, and sign up for a course in your chosen field, just make sure you don't stop acquiring new knowledge.

I believe in you.

DAY 26
YOUR PURPOSE IS NOT FAR FROM YOU

When I was young, I would watch Evangelist Reinhard Bonnke on VHS. My parents, since the age of 7 or 8, would play it all day long. When others were watching Rambo and Turtle Ninja, we were watching Reinhard Bonnke, R.W. Schambach, Benny Hinn, etc.

Since that age, whenever people asked me what I wanted to do when I grew up, I always answered, 'n Evangelist.' I was so inspired to the extent that when I had my interview for High School (after passing my Common Entrance Examination), they asked me which school I wanted to go to, and I said, 'Missionary School.'

Since there was no missionary school owned by the government in Northern Nigeria, they wrote 'missionary school' in my report and I discovered I was not placed in any school. It was when my parents went to enquire about why I was not placed in any school that they were told: 'Our son wants to go to missionary school.'

It is no surprise today, to the glory of God, that I am a preacher and teacher.

Your purpose is not far from you. It is usually the very thing you have desired to do as a child. The cue is not very far away from you. The truth is, every child has what they want to do or be when they grow older, but life ambitions can be tempting at times. There are lots of older people right now who are feeling so sad about what they could have done or started years ago that they couldn't do. The pressure of life has taken away their time, they can not figure anything out again and they are wondering if they could get another chance of starting what they had been dreaming of starting years ago.

I know that now the pressures of life and realities that come with them may have shrunk that desire but don't let that stop you. Don't think you are too old to do it or go back to school to learn about it. You are not too old and it is not too late for you. Your purpose will always be on you; you may run away to the south or the west, but it will always be with you. It is not far from you and you are not far from it. You can do well to embrace your original purpose right now and begin to live in it. Your age and status don't matter, what matters the most is your availability. If you are available for what God has called and created you to do, then He will empower you to do it.

You are better for it if you start living a purposeful life; everything God is asking you to do is for your good, not necessarily for God's good. You are not doing God a favour if you are doing purpose, but you are doing yourself a lot of good because there is a reward for you at the end. Your purpose is attached to you, don't run from it, don't excuse yourself, and don't neglect it.

Don't be like Jonah who was trying to run away from his purpose, but even though he ran, his purpose still caught up with him and he later fulfilled it. You also should gear yourself up and begin from where you are. Start living a purposeful life. It is never too late to get back on the track of purpose, it is never too late to become who you were born and created to be.

Get back on that path of purpose today.

Don't worry about what anyone thinks.

Do what you have always loved to do.

If you enjoy inspiring people, start doing it right away. If you love teaching, start teaching right away. If you enjoy flying, enroll in aviation school. If you love to write books, why not start writing and publish your first book even at your age? You are not too late and you are not too early. If you love to cook, then start cooking, and start selling your food. Someone is still waiting for the best eatery out there, they might just be waiting for you. It is not too late to start singing, someone from somewhere might be blessed with your music.

One act of obedience will save you and save lots of other people, while your disobedience can make someone you don't even know lose their life. Get on the track right away and start doing something with what God has called you to do. You will be better for it.

I believe in you.

DAY 27

THE ALTITUDE OF GREATNESS

The surest path to greatness is service.

Have the attitude of a servant.

Choose to serve the people God has brought into your life.

Serve your spouse.

Serve your Pastor.

Serve at work.

Serve your community.

Serve in church.

Let everything about you ring service.

Each day, God presents you with an opportunity to serve and be a blessing to someone.

You may not even know them, but do what you can, what you can afford, to serve them.

You may not have money, but you can inspire them. You may not have a relationship with them but you can smile at them. You may not have what they need but you can give what you have. Do your best to serve others, not because they deserve it but because you need to.

Well, you may say, 'I don't have anything to offer or give.' That's a lie from the pit of hell. You will always have something to give. Regardless of who you are, you will always have something; you are not empty, you are always with something. This is the truth, it is not how much that you have that matters when it comes to giving, it is how much you are willing to sacrifice out of the little you have.

One thing about service is that you will always have one thing to offer people. Even God gave us His only son, so who are you not to give others the only thing you have? If you desire to be great, then be ready to live a life of sacrifice, you must be willing to offer something and serve others. You can't be great without being useful in one way or the other to some people.

Mark Zuckerberg, the founder of Facebook, and others only wanted to connect with one or two people in their community. The guy just wanted to serve, he wanted to offer something to his community, he wanted to bless them with something, and this one thing later became the world's project. There is nowhere in a civilized country that people are not using

Facebook, Instagram, and probably Thread. That's what I'm talking about, your greatness is tied to how much you are willing to serve others.

There is no way you will genuinely serve others and not be great. Jesus came to the world to serve the world, not to be served by the world. Are you also willing to serve? Then start serving; recognise who you want to serve, identify how you want to serve them, and start. No matter how little you think of yourself, there will always be something unique and different about you. You are not empty, you are loaded with something, and you must start offering it as a service. Always remember that the altitude of greatness is the attitude of your greatness.

Jesus said, 'He that is greatest among you shall be your servant.' To be great, we don't look to be served, we become servants. The attitude of service determines your altitude of greatness.

I believe in you.

DAY 28

VALUE

Recently, I was invited somewhere to speak and on my last day in the city, I was checking out of my hotel when the hotel attendant asked me to sign on a piece of paper.

I looked at it, and it was the invoice for my hotel. Up until then, I had no idea about the cost of hosting me at the hotel. Well, my mouth was agape when I saw the invoice, yet my heart was filled with so much gratitude. I know I am nowhere near where I want and dream to be, but for where I am now, I am extremely grateful.

As I write this, I am aboard a plane to another city for another speaking engagement.

And over the last few minutes, I've been asking myself, why do people and organisations spend money to book and pay me and other great speakers to speak at their events, churches, and corporate organisations?

As I reflected on this question, I got a realisation. It is not like these people or organisations like my face so much that they want to see me. Well, I know they do but they won't pay me because they just love me, would they? I don't think so. They are not paying to see my handsome face (I know I am very handsome, no doubt. Hahaha!)

So, what are they paying for? Value! I realised that they were paying for what I carry. They are paying for my gift. They recognise it, they see it, it meets their needs and they would pay to have it. See, earlier on in my life when these trips were still a dream deep inside me, I often wonder if people will ever pay me to do what I love to do.

Now, it's happening. It's amazing.

Why am I sharing this?

I am sharing this for the following reasons:

1. Your gift is the source of your value. Your job is not the source of your value but your gift. Spend more time working on your gift than you do working on your job. I have seen people who work from 9 to 5, spend most of their time on their job, but they are not paying attention to their gift. Most of these people are frustrated and not happy. Deep down they want something that could make them happy, and fulfilled, but they are not ready to leave their job. The truth about me

is that the people that are inviting me are not paying me for the job I'm doing for them, they are rather paying me for the gift that I carry.

You also have something that people can pay for, you have a gift on your inside, God deliberately gave you those gifts and He wants you to make use of what you have to get what you want. Your gift is your source of value, you must start making use of it. Your 9 to 5 job may not be able to keep and sustain you for the rest of your life, but your gift will do that for you.

2. People will not pay you because you are beautiful or handsome, they will pay you because of what you carry. They will look for you because of your gift. People don't just give money away because they are not Father Christmas. People will give you money because you offer them value. To remain relevant in people's lives, you must consistently do something for them that will keep that relevance. To make people pay you for something, you must also give them something that they can pay for.

Someone will not just come to you and give you money because you have a fair complexion, people won't just throw money at you because you are tall, handsome, and have six packs. Six-packs without any spark of value are just an ordinary amusement park. You must discover your packs of value and offer people what you've gotten on your inside.

3. Even if your gift isn't bringing you anything now, don't quit. Gold often takes time in the fire before it becomes refined

and recognised as gold. Keep working on yourself. There have been several people who gave up on the verge of their breakthrough. Just because people don't recognise or know you for what you are doing at the moment doesn't mean you should give up. You must consistently work on your gift; it is your consistency that will bring breakthroughs into your life. Don't give up on your gift, keep at it, continue doing it, and very soon, you will see the result of all you're doing.

4. Always be grateful for where you are on your journey. You may not be where you want to be yet but you are not where you once were. Don't complain about your present level, continue to live a life of gratitude. One thing about gratitude is that it opens closed doors.

Your life's journey is peculiar and unique, you should thank God for your progress even if it is little. Always remember it is little progress that does turn into bigger ones. You may not be on the winning side today, but if you don't quit, you will be on the winning side tomorrow. It is simply a journey, it is not a destination. That you are not where you wish to be today doesn't mean you won't get there tomorrow.

5. Always seek to become a person of value. It's the fastest way to the top. To be a person of value, you must consistently be working on making yourself a better person. You must consistently sharpen your skills, this will make you a person of great value. If you want to get to the top early in life, then you must seek to be the best at what you are doing. In seeking to

serve great men, mediocrity is not allowed. You must be good at what you are doing, even if you are not perfect yet, just make sure you are good.

'Then she gave the king one hundred and twenty talents of gold, spices in great quantity, and precious stones. There never again came such abundance of spices as the queen of Sheba gave to King Solomon.' 1 Kings 10:10 NKJV.

Solomon was a very wise man and because of this, he became a sought-after man. People came from afar, from different countries, to listen to his wealth of wisdom. He always had solutions to people's problems. Even the Queen of Sheba came for him from another country. She brought gifts for Solomon. She did not bring those gifts to Solomon because she felt Solomon was a good man, or handsome. No, she brought those gifts because she perceived value. When people perceive that you are a person of value, they will be willing to pay you for what you can offer.

I believe in you.

DAY 29

SUCCESS IS A LIFESTYLE

When I got my Ph.D. at the age of 26, it felt like the best thing I could ever achieve. I was proud of the degree and grateful for it but I knew and still know that's only just the beginning.

Hear this, success is not an attainment; it's a lifestyle. Success is not a destination but a journey. It is not a sprint but a marathon. You cannot arrive at the destination called success; you will always have to stay on that journey. It is harder to stay successful than to be successful. This is why successful people are always improving. Life, for a successful person, is a succession of daily improvements.

You assess your life, make the required changes, see results, and continue that cycle.

To think your success in life is defined by a single achievement or a series of achievements, you are wrong. Success is progressive, successful people understand this and this is why they will always get better each day so that they will beat the record of yesterday.

Yesterday's success is gone and if you want to achieve more success, you must forget about what you have achieved yesterday and focus on what you will achieve in the future. Don't think you are already successful at what you are doing. No, you are not, you are just on the way. I tell people not to feel complacent at the achievement of new successes. Many good things are stored in the future for you, and you must achieve them. If you don't forget yesterday's successes, you will not go for tomorrow's successes.

Make success your normal lifestyle, let it be normal for you to succeed, with this, you will always beat your yesterday's result. The success mentality must always be on you, this will enable you to be on track always and won't make you fall.

Some people have this mentality that they have automatically 'arrived' when they achieve a small success. That's a loser mentality! That's a mediocre mindset! Don't think like that! If you have been thinking like that before now; stop it! Don't trap yourself in the cage of arrival mentality. Many are yet to recover from it to date because they eventually lost everything they have ever worked for. Yesterday's success is relevant only if you can work harder and build on it. Yesterday's success will only be relevant if you intentionally make success your usual lifestyle.

Success is not a destination.

Purpose is not a destination.

Purpose is a journey, and so is success.

I believe in you.

DAY 30

THE POWER OF RELATIONSHIPS

Do you know that 85% of your happiness in life will be determined by the quality of your relationships?

Why then do you joke with your relationships?

Why are you not intentional about who you spend time with?

Why are you not careful about your attitude to those around you?

Relationships are like plants. You must intentionally cultivate them to get the best out of them. Learn how to keep good and productive people around your life. Stop sending people out of your life, learn the act of making relationships work. Every one God has planted into your life is there for certain reasons, and you must do everything in your capacity to keep and nurture them.

The truth is that relationships play pivotal roles on the journey to your next level and destiny. In the economy of success and breakthroughs, you can't do without having or keeping quality relationships because it is capital. I can even say that relationships are part of the currency that people are spending to get into their place of fulfilment. Your network in this life will also determine your net worth. Anytime God wants to help or lift you, He will position the right set of people along your path because God also knows you can't fulfill destiny all alone. This was one of the reasons He gave Eve to Adam. He knew Adam couldn't live a fulfilled life all alone.

Relationships are so important. Keeping relationships, especially with those who can positively impact your life, will do you lots of good. One thing you should do is to intentionally recognise good relationships around your life and stick to them. Move with quality people and everything about you will also be quality. If you continue to move with mediocre people, your life will soon look like theirs.

Relationships are important and you must be intentional about cultivating them. In most cases, relationships don't automatically work out, you must bid for it and make it work out. In other words, if you leave your relationships to chance, you are likely to reap nothing or weeds.

For every plant we seek fruits from, we have to weed them regularly, water them when required, and make sure they get the nutrients necessary for them to grow and blossom.

The same applies to good relationships in your life. You must nurture the people God has placed in your life. When was the last time you said, 'Thank you.' to your Pastor? When was the last time you bought his wife a gift? When was the last time you added value to the life of your mentor? When was the last time you gave back to those who have been blessing your life and helping you become better?

See, if you don't feed what feeds you, that source will soon dry up. If you don't nurture the soil for your plant, it will soon wither and you will have nothing to show.

Any relationship you don't give to will not benefit you for long. Relationships are powerful; just as they can act as a ladder to greatness, they can bring one into the mud. This is why you must be intentional and also know the kind of relationship you will allow into your life.

We've mostly been discussing fulfilling your purpose, discovering your gifts, potential, and so on in this book. But do you know that you won't be able to live a fulfilled life without having good people around you? This is because purpose is not fulfilled in isolation, you must do it with other people and you must be intentional about building it - I mean good relationships.

Ultimately, your success in life may not necessarily be determined by your gifts or potential, it would also be determined by the relationships you've chosen to keep and nurture around your life. There are lots of talented people dying in obscurity today, not because they are not gifted or good, but because they have decided to stay and be alone. You can't choose to stay alone, you should build a system around other people, this will make you grow and develop and also help you go faster to your destination.

Meanwhile, every relationship must be built on the platform of value giving. If you are not giving any value in a given relationship, you will lose the respect of the other, and with that, you may lose your credibility in that relationship. As far as I am concerned, I believe that value has to be two-sided.

If you are just receiving without giving back, it will backfire on you one day. The question I want to ask is, are you just receiving and not giving back? Don't be like that. Check yourself and make amends.

To fulfil purpose effectively, you must add value to what and whoever is adding value to you.

Can I get an 'Amen?

I believe in you.

www.ingramcontent.com/pod-product-compliance
Lightning Source LLC
LaVergne TN
LVHW091555060526
838200LV00036B/843